A Teen
Eating Disorder
Prevention
Book

Understanding Recovery from Eating Disorders

Toni L. Rocha

The Rosen Publishing Group, Inc./New York

Published in 1999 by The Rosen Publishing Group, Inc.
29 East 21st Street, New York, NY 10010

Library of Congress Cataloging-in-Publication Data

Rocha, Toni L.
    Understanding recovery from eating disorders / Toni
L. Rocha. — 1st ed.
        p. cm. — (Teen eating disorder prevention book)
    Includes bibliographical references and index.
    Summary: Discusses different eating disorders includ-
ing bulimia, anorexia, and compulsive exercise. Also describes
some of the warning signals and physical symptoms of each
disorder and the recovery process.
    ISBN 0-8239-2884-5
    1. Eating disorders—Juvenile literature. 2. Anorexia
nervosa—Juvenile literature. 3. Bulimia—Juvenile literature.
[1. Eating disorders. 2. Exercise addiction.] I. Title.
II. Series.
RC552.E18R63   1999
616.85'26—dc21   99-26582
                                                  CIP

Manufactured in the United States of America

ABOUT THE AUTHOR

Toni L. Rocha recently retired from her position as police and fire reporter for the Beloit Daily News in Beloit, Wisconsin. With more than thirty years of experience writing in various areas of the communications field, including advertising, she is now writing freelance out of her home in Roscoe, Illinois.

ACKNOWLEDGMENTS

A writer rarely creates anything worthwhile without the input and advice of others. This writer is no exception.

This book could not exist without the courageous contributions of "Wendy," "Linda," and "Randy." These characterizations were based on the true experiences of young adults who are successfully recovering from eating disorders.

I owe considerable thanks to dedicated librarians at the North Suburban Library in Loves Park, Illinois, and the Roscoe Branch Library in Roscoe, Illinois, who spent time and effort helping me research eating disorders. I also owe sincere appreciation to my editor, Amy Haugesag, whose professionalism and patience helped me complete this assignment with most of my wits still intact.

To my husband, Robert,
who never lost faith in my
ability to write.

Contents

Introduction: Karen's Legacy

"We've only just begun to live..."

The opening lyrics from The Carpenters' second gold record seem prophetic, don't they? In 1970, when "We've Only Just Begun" was a hit, it would have been easy to believe that the Carpenters—a brother-sister pop duo who were immensely talented and recognized worldwide for their distinctive sound—would remain near the top of the record charts for years to come.

That ended with Karen's unexpected death on February 4, 1983, after an eight-year battle with multiple eating disorders. She was thirty-two years old.

Little was known about Karen's eating disorder in 1975, when her family and fans began to realize something was terribly wrong. As her weight dropped below one hundred pounds, a European and Japanese tour had to be canceled; Karen tired too easily to perform two daily shows as the contracts required. Karen was hospitalized for anorexia

1

for five days and spent the next two months in bed at her parents' home.

"Mainly we just encouraged her to eat more. We never knew how to help her," Karen's brother Richard told *People* magazine in an interview nine months after Karen's death. "In late 1981, she reached the stage where she came to me and said, 'Richard, I realize I'm sick and I need help.'"

Richard also commented to *People* that Karen had purchased thirty pairs of jogging shoes while being treated for anorexia in New York. It's clear now that Karen was also fighting compulsive exercise disorder, another method of losing weight that often overlaps anorexia and bulimia.

After more than a year of therapy and a two-month hospitalization, Karen had gained twenty-four pounds. Outwardly, she appeared to have overcome the anorexia and laxative addiction she had fought for nearly eight years. Her death from heart failure stunned the world and focused an intense spotlight on the shadowy world of eating disorders.

At first, medical experts attributed her unexpected death to low potassium levels in the blood, which can cause irregular heartbeat—a serious condition for someone whose heart has already been damaged by years of slow starvation. But after her death, the medical examiner concluded that Karen had actually died from emetine poisoning, which caused her heart to stop beating.

You've never heard of it? That's not surprising. Emetine, which comes from the root of a South American plant, is the main ingredient in syrup of ipecac. A dark brown, foul-smelling liquid, ipecac is used to induce vomiting in people who have swallowed poison. But ipecac is a poison itself, and if it is taken too often or in large doses, it can cause irreversible heart damage.

A normal dose of ipecac is a teaspoon or so, depending on a person's age and size. Karen's therapist, Dr. Steven Levenkron, says she must have been swallowing several teaspoons every night after dinner, gradually increasing her intake to as much as a bottle or two daily.

So it seems that after overcoming anorexia, compulsive exercise syndrome, and laxative addiction, Karen began misusing ipecac to help control her weight. She developed another type of eating disorder, bulimia nervosa, in which people eat normal to excessive amounts of food, then force themselves to vomit to prevent weight gain.

People with anorexia eat very little or refuse to eat at all. People with bulimia may eat what seems to be a normal amount of food or even overeat. But then they find a way to induce vomiting to rid themselves of the food they have taken in. Karen had survived anorexia and was well along in the recovery process. Evidence that she had somehow slipped into bulimic behavior indicates how difficult recovery from an eating disorder can be.

You might be surprised to learn that Karen took time out from her busy recording and performance schedule to help others who were recovering from eating disorders. Because a person with an eating disorder tends to deny there's a problem, and is often secretive about it as well, Karen's courage to reach beyond her personal struggle with anorexia and encourage others was especially meaningful.

Dr. Levenkron told *People* that after leaving the hospital, Karen had called the girls she met there to encourage them. "She wanted people to know anorexia could be cured," he said.

This book is designed to help you understand more about eating disorders and what is involved in the recovery process. You will learn the warning signals and physical symptoms of anorexia nervosa, bulimia and binge-purge syndrome, binge eating, compulsive eating, compulsive exercise and muscular dysmorphia.

You will also meet three young adults who are in the recovery process: Wendy, who became anorexic at age four; Linda, whose battle with bulimia is ongoing; and Randy, a member of Overeaters Anonymous, who is overcoming compulsive eating disorder.

Like Karen Carpenter, they are willing to reach out to others their age, to help them understand what it means to face and overcome eating disorders. As they share their stories and insights, you will discover how puzzling and difficult these disorders are to reverse.

You'll also hear from many medical professionals who treat these difficult disorders. They will talk about the latest treatment methods and what the experts have discovered in their efforts to help their patients recover.

Most important, you'll know more about these complicated psychological disorders. You'll understand why food plays a very small part in the onset of and recovery from them, compared to such powerful influences as self-image, self-esteem, denial, and possible physical causes. And finally, you'll understand better why these disorders must be recognized and treated.

Introduction

Karen Carpenter gave her listening public something just as important as her music. Her highly visible battle to overcome anorexia at a time when it was relatively unknown brought the dark, scary world of eating disorders into the light. Thanks to Karen, and to thousands more who are working to develop successful recovery programs, eating disorders are becoming better understood and better treated.

PART 1

The ABCs of Eating Disorders

1 Myths and Misconceptions

"**R**ecovery from an eating disorder is like looking through a kaleidoscope," says Janet B. DeBruyne, a licensed clinical counselor for the SwedishAmerican Center for Mental Health in Rockford, Illinois. "Move one little piece, and the entire pattern changes."

It would be easy to believe that eating disorders are all about food, but that isn't the case. Instead, they are psychological conditions in which eating behavior is only one fragment of a complex mystery.

Low self-esteem—a lack of confidence in oneself and one's abilities—seems to be a key element of eating disorders. A poor or unrealistic self-image is another important factor. So are striving for perfection, denying that anything is wrong, and a person's need to feel in control of at least one aspect of his or her life. People with eating disorders tend to be sweet-tempered, soft-spoken, and generous, often taking better care of others than they do of themselves.

Another troubling aspect of many eating disorders

is the presence of a dominating person, most often a parent, who takes more control over the person's life than is necessary or healthy. Anorexics, for example, are usually the children of authoritative parents. They are obedient children and are not inclined to rebel.

Although medical professionals have learned a great deal about the symptoms and side effects of eating disorders in the past twenty years, they still don't understand why one person develops an eating disorder whereas another with the same background and characteristics does not. The true cause of eating disorders—if there is a single cause—has yet to be discovered, and it's important to keep searching.

The American Anorexia/Bulimia Association, Inc. (AABA), estimates that more than five million Americans have some form of eating disorder. That may not sound like a lot until you understand that 5 percent of adolescent and adult women and 1 percent of adolescent and adult men have anorexia nervosa, bulimia nervosa, or binge-eating disorders. Another 15 percent of young women exhibit substantially disordered eating attitudes and behaviors, meaning that although they do not have full-fledged eating disorders, their attitudes and actions related to food and their bodies are not normal.

Worse, an estimated one thousand young women die each year from anorexia nervosa as the result of starvation, permanent damage to their vital organs, or suicide.

As with most psychologically based illnesses, eating disorders can't be "cured." The behaviors become an integral part of the person's character patterns once they have been acted upon. In other words, you can't forget you had an eating disorder. There are no magic pills or potions to erase an eating disorder from the brain's memory. The recovery process is ongoing and requires support through professional therapy, antidepressant and anti-anxiety medications, and lifelong vigilance.

INTRODUCING THE ABCs OF EATING DISORDERS

Eating disorders are classified as psychiatric illnesses because they are as much a product of perception as they are a physical condition. Despite the many elements involved, eating disorders do generally break down into recognizable groups.

The fact that eating disorders are psychiatric illnesses does not mean that eating disorders are considered psychosomatic. A psychosomatic disease is one that a person imagines he or she has but does not actually have. Eating disorders are very real, even though part of the eating disorder is caused by a distorted perception of self-worth and self-image.

In a psychosomatic condition, the person might believe he or she has a serious illness, but there is no physical evidence to support that belief. With eating disorders, the physical symptoms are measurable and very real. And the end result of untreated eating disorders is just as serious and potentially fatal as a purely physical disease that is left untreated.

Anorexia Nervosa

Anorexia nervosa is an eating disorder in which the individual is preoccupied with food, dieting, and thinness to the point of starvation. A person is diagnosed with anorexia nervosa if he or she weighs less than 85 percent of the expected body weight for his or her age, height, and physical build. Denial, low self-esteem, unrealistic self-image, fear of growing up, and perfectionism are some of the known reasons that a person might develop anorexia nervosa. It is by far the most dangerous of the eating disorders. You'll learn more about this dangerous, sometimes fatal, eating disorder from Wendy in chapter two.

Bulimia and Binge-Purge Syndrome

Bulimia and binge-purge syndrome are two separate but related eating disorders in which a person eats, then purges, or gets rid of the food through induced vomiting and/or habitual use of laxatives, which cause the user to defecate, and diuretics, which make the user urinate frequently.

The differences between bulimia and binge-purge syndrome lie in the amount of food eaten, how often the person purges, and in some respects, physical appearance. With bulimia, a person may eat normally or ingest a lot of food all at once before inducing vomiting or taking laxatives or diuretics. And with bulimia, the behavior is almost always a daily routine, with vomiting induced one or more times each day. Also, a bulimic may be of normal weight or slightly above normal.

In binge-purge syndrome, the person may eat huge amounts of food within a relatively short period of time, generally about two hours. Then vomiting is induced. This may take place as often as two to three times a week, but not on a daily basis. Laxatives and diuretics are also used to help rid the body of the excess food, as is fasting. A person with binge-purge syndrome tends to be slightly overweight.

The wide swings between eating, fasting, and purging take a serious toll on the person's body. Reading Linda's story in chapter three will help you understand more about bulimia and binge-purge syndrome.

Compulsive Eating and Binge Eating

Compulsive eaters, along with overweight binge eaters, experience uncontrolled bouts of eating. They may be secret eaters as well.

The compulsive overeater suffers almost daily bouts of uncontrolled eating, whereas the binge eater may go for days without any symptoms of this eating disorder before succumbing to the urge to eat huge amounts of food. Neither of these types of eating disorders involves purging, although the person may make a conscientious effort to reduce his or her food intake between eating bouts.

Medical professionals suspect as much as 40 percent of obese people (extremely overweight) may be binge or compulsive eaters. Depression, feelings of helplessness or hopelessness, and other psychological problems often influence the onset of these disorders and make them difficult to overcome. The description of Randy's experiences in chapter four will help you understand more about compulsive and binge eating.

Compulsive Exercise Disorder

You've always heard that exercise is essential to a healthy body. But some people seem to get caught up in a vicious cycle to burn calories and control their weight as well as other aspects of their lives. Compulsive exercise disorder is often a companion to compulsive overeating, but it has been noted in people with anorexia and bulimia as well. In chapter five, you'll read about the difference between healthy and unhealthy amounts of exercise and why it's important to separate exercise from weight control.

One of the cruelest aspects of eating disorders is that they often overlap in one person. For example, an anorexic person may use bulimic behaviors as a way of further reducing his or her weight. That person may also begin exercising excessively for the same reason. Add the overuse of harsh laxatives and diuretics, and you've created a complex pattern that can take months and even years to overcome.

WATCH FOR THE DANGER SIGNS OF AN EATING DISORDER

When a person with an eating disorder is first recovering, she still follows destructive eating patterns. The initial stage of recovery can take as little as four months or longer than a year. During that time, permanent damage to internal organs such as the heart, lungs, brain, liver, kidneys, and stomach can occur. That's why it's important to recognize the signs of an eating disorder early and begin treatment as quickly as possible.

The American Dietetic Association (ADA) lists the following eleven warning signs to watch for:

1. Eating tiny portions or refusing food. Sometimes the person pushes the food around on the plate to make it appear as if he or she has eaten some of it. People with eating disorders even hide food beneath a napkin or throw it on the floor under the table. They share food too easily, giving up more than half and then finding ways to hide the fact that they aren't eating what they've kept. They

often repeat the phrase "I'm not hungry," and make excuses not to sit down at the table for family meals.

2. Quick weight loss or gain without any other cause. When a person begins eating too much or stops eating altogether, it doesn't take long for the effects to show. If someone you know suddenly gains or loses a lot of weight with no logical explanation (such as illness or increased physical activity), there's good reason to be concerned about a possible eating disorder. You should be especially concerned if the person denies that anything is wrong.

3. Intense and irrational fears of becoming overweight. Anorexia and bulimia can result from an unrealistic self-image or a deep-seated need to be perfect. The person may become obsessive about how small his or her waist is or how slim the arms and legs are. He or she might spend a lot of time in front of the mirror, trying on clothes to see how they

fit, or weigh himself or herself several times every day, especially after eating something.

4. Excessive exercising. You know that one healthy way to control weight is to exercise regularly. But that good habit can be taken to extremes by a person with an eating disorder who is trying to lose weight. Someone who signs up for several exercise classes daily, obsessively walks for miles, or spends hours pedaling energetically on a stationary bicycle may have compulsive exercise disorder.

5. Eating secretly and hiding food. Some anorexics believe that they do not deserve to eat, and they hide what few bites of food they do take from anyone who might see them eat. But this warning sign is most likely to be seen in people who are either compulsive overeaters or binge eaters. They eat secretly, getting up in the middle of the night or finding places where they can eat large quantities of food without being discovered.

They keep food in their cars, in their bedrooms, or even in the bathroom, stockpiled and waiting for the time when they can escape from family and friends to eat.

6. Disappearing after meals, often into a bathroom. This behavior is most often seen in people with bulimia nervosa. The bulimic eats a normal to large amount of food, then immediately excuses himself or herself from the table and goes directly to the bathroom, locking the door. Often the person remains in the bathroom for long periods of time. Other bulimics may go for a long walk or drive after each meal. You might even find that they get up in the middle of the night and spend an unusually long time in the bathroom. Most often, however, it happens right after the person has eaten.

7. Loss of menstrual cycle. A woman with an eating disorder will eventually stop menstruating. Extreme loss of weight can cause normal body functions to

falter or cease altogether (as can extremely large weight gains). Sporadic or total loss of menstrual cycles can occur in women athletes who must keep their weight down to perform competitively, and it also occurs among some performing artists, such as ballet dancers. Anorexia is mainly the cause of this symptom.

8. Dependency on laxatives, diuretics, or diet pills. Like other drugs, these chemicals can become addictive if overused. You are not likely to find evidence of too much reliance on laxatives, diuretics, or diet pills in the medicine cabinet, since people with this dependency are usually secretive about their behavior, but watching the personal habits of anyone who overuses them can tip you off. Once again, the person may spend a lot more time than normal in the bathroom. He or she may become dehydrated from taking laxatives or diuretics and not drinking enough water or other

fluids. Diet pills can also make users jittery and nervous, talk more than they normally would, or even make them irritable and argumentative.

9. Significant fluctuations in weight. Sudden or constant changes in weight may be the result of two different behaviors. The person may be a binge eater whose eating pattern includes regular bouts of extreme overeating that last for several days, after which the weight is lost, only to be put on again with the next binge. Or the person may be bulimic on an inconsistent basis—eating until she or he feels too much weight has been gained and then using bulimic behavior to lose the weight.

10. Unusual preoccupation with food. Oddly, people with anorexia nervosa may spend a lot of time talking about food and restaurants, reading recipes in cookbooks and magazines, and planning menus to serve to family and friends—featuring

food they have no intention of eating themselves. They may carry calorie counters, fat-gram guides, or other diet and nutritional books around with them and study the information constantly.

11. Development of strange eating rituals. This behavior can range from sudden avoidance of foods that the person normally likes to eating unappetizing mixtures of food, hiding the act of eating behind a hand or napkin, refusing to eat certain foods together, and other inexplicable changes in eating habits.

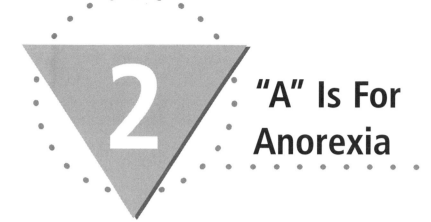

2 "A" Is For Anorexia

If you looked closely at Wendy, you would realize she isn't healthy. Perhaps you wouldn't be able to put your finger on exactly why, but somehow you would know. What you wouldn't understand without being told is that Wendy is slowly recovering from a thirty-one-year struggle with anorexia nervosa.

"I actually became anorexic at about four years of age," Wendy says. "I remember it so well because it was a terribly hard time for me. I was being molested by a distant member of my family. My father and I argued, sometimes all night, about my refusal to eat. The problem was I didn't trust my parents enough to tell them what was really wrong."

Wendy says that when she was young, she believed she had to be perfect, and she put a lot of pressure on herself to succeed. At the same time, Wendy believed she had no one to protect her, and that she had no control over her life.

"I felt as if I had been abandoned," Wendy says. "Many anorexics do. The only control I had was my weight. When I didn't eat, I won. That feeling is so deeply ingrained in me that it's still difficult to over-come some days."

Wendy graduated from college and found an excellent job at which she earned a lot of respect. Her chosen profession was demanding, and the pressure Wendy continued to put on herself to be perfect con-tributed to her ongoing anorexic behavior.

As her weight dropped to less than seventy-five pounds, Wendy allowed herself to eat just half an orange a day for weeks at a time. Finally, she became so ill that she admitted to herself she had a problem. By that time, Wendy was twenty-nine years old and wasting away in front of her family's and friends' eyes. She was no longer able to func-tion at work.

GETTING HELP

"I started seeing a psychiatrist," Wendy says. "The first thing he did was confront me with the fact that I was anorexic. No one had ever done that before. It scared me so badly, I balked and refused to talk to him."

Then the doctor did something Wendy didn't expect. "He gave me his home telephone number and told me that when I was ready to talk, he'd be ready and waiting to listen," Wendy says. "I know doctors don't usually do that. He really gave me something new to think about."

After thinking it over carefully, Wendy says, she decided to enter a treatment program. "It was a long, hard process," Wendy says. "I spent nine weeks in that first program. During that time, I needed surgery [for an unrelated problem]. That's when I learned firsthand what twenty-five years of anorexia had done to my body."

Severe lack of vitamin K prevented Wendy's blood from clotting. Intravenous feeding and medications made her starved body swell painfully. And still, she refused to eat.

"My doctor went through hell for me," Wendy says. "He was by my side at all hours. Finally, he said, 'Look, I've stood behind you all the way, and I always will. Do me a favor and please eat.'"

Wendy realized how concerned her doctor was and how much he was trying to help her. She began to participate in the program wholeheartedly, doing physical therapy and gaining weight until she reached 105 pounds. Wendy was discharged after her nine-week session but continued outpatient treatment on a daily basis.

"I had moved back in with my parents at that time," Wendy says. "Things were terrible at home. I was too sick to live alone, and that seemed to frighten my parents. We fell back into the same old pattern as when I was a child . . . my refusing to eat properly and my father screaming at me all night. Poor Mom tried to make peace and usually ended up in the middle, getting yelled at by both of us."

Wendy became extremely depressed. The atmosphere at home seemed to completely negate all the progress she'd made at the hospital. "I thought about taking an overdose of the lithium that I was taking, because I was so miserable that I wanted to die," Wendy says.

Instead, Wendy packed her things at four o'clock in the morning and voluntarily checked herself back into the hospital. There, she was placed in isolation on Thorazine, a strong sedative. "I didn't want anyone to come near me or even touch me," Wendy says. "It was one of the lowest points in my whole life."

With her condition somewhat stable, Wendy decided to act on her doctor's advice that she commit herself to at least a year of highly specialized treatment for her anorexia at a university medical facility in Chicago.

"That was a grueling experience," Wendy explains. "I was under twenty-four-hour observation. Every single thing I ate, even every time I went to the bathroom, someone was there. Part of the treatment involved working on my diet and learning nutrition. Each of us had to plan our menus daily. It was one thing to plan a meal, but quite another to eat it."

For every morsel of food she refused to eat, Wendy had to drink a serving of Sustacal, a nutritional supplement. Because she had entered treatment voluntarily, Wendy could be kicked out if she didn't do what was expected of her. "I finally got so angry and frustrated, I spent five days lying on the windowsill in my room, wrapped in a blanket," Wendy says. "I kept the blinds closed and sat in the dark, day and night."

At the end of five days, Wendy's doctor marched into her room, yanked the blinds open and told her, "Don't you pull this on me, Wendy. Cut the theatrics and get out from under those covers!"

"He was the only one to challenge me," Wendy says. "The program was strict, but we were part of an elite unit. My fellow patients were professionals and even entertainers. You'd be amazed at who was in that unit some of the time."

THE JOURNEY TO RECOVERY

For too many, Wendy says, anorexia seems to be a death wish. For those who survive, it's a journey of self-discovery.

"I learned a lot on that unit," Wendy stresses. "We participated in group sessions that included people who weighed more than four hundred pounds. They'd look at us as if they wanted to kill us, and we'd look at them and wonder, 'How could you do this to yourself?'"

But while her attitude was gradually changing for the better, Wendy's physical health continued to fail. She began to vomit up much of what she ate at each meal because her digestive system's normal functions had begun to fail. This wasn't bulimic behavior on Wendy's part. Instead, the vomiting was her body's response to no longer being able to handle any amount of food. Test after test was conducted to determine what was wrong. "Through it all, my doctor never gave up on me," Wendy says, "no matter how awful I was. We were in a locked unit with no freedom and no choices. It was easy to get angry and take it out on the doctors and nurses. I know it sounds childish, but for me, it was that old issue: lack of control."

Part of the recovery process involved family therapy sessions, which Wendy describes as extremely emotional. They left her drained and feeling that more pressure was being put on her than she could bear at times. But Wendy's sense of humor triumphed on occasion.

"I remember one night when there were only two regulars on the unit, me and another woman,"

Wendy says. "The new patients, all between the ages of thirteen and fifteen, ordered fish because they thought it would get them in good with the observers. We regulars knew better. The fish there was awful! We ordered omelets."

Wendy told the new patients that homeless people who slept under a nearby river bridge picked up all the dead fish from the shoreline and sold them to the hospital kitchen. As she finished her omelet, Wendy watched the new girls, as one by one, they laid down their forks and refused to eat the fish.

"Every one of them had to drink Sustacal," Wendy says, laughing. "The nurse said it was the most disgusting thing she'd ever heard. But a good laugh was one of the best ways to deal with the program. You had to be able to laugh."

Sadly, Wendy adds, nearly every one of the young patients in her unit was intelligent, sensitive, and artistic. "It's very strange how we get so far off track," she says.

"At thirty-four, I was one of the oldest patients on the unit," Wendy says. "When the younger patients saw how sick I was and learned how long I'd been there, they gained weight and got out fast. I scared them to death."

Wendy has completed more than ten years of treatment and still talks with her doctor three times each week. She weighs ninety-eight pounds, which is less than she should weigh, but she has gone back to work and lives on her own.

"People never understand how long-term anorexia messes up your system," Wendy says. "I'll continue to recover, but only to a certain point. It takes its toll in the end. There is no truly complete recovery, and that's what young people don't understand."

Today, Wendy continues to struggle with ultra-low potassium levels in her blood, which damages muscles, and low blood pressure. She has already suffered a heart attack and will probably have to have dialysis in the future, because after years of dehydration and vitamin deficiencies, her kidneys are failing. These health problems are all due to the effects of anorexia on Wendy's body.

Other ongoing symptoms of anorexia Wendy has to this day include frequent headaches from low blood pressure and not enough oxygen being supplied to her brain. Wendy says she almost always feels cold, and often her heart beats painfully fast and irregularly. Tingling in her hands, feet, arms, toes, and lips are another cause of discomfort. Her teeth are a constant source of trouble and pain, but Wendy can't have oral surgery now because of her weakened physical condition. Her skin is extremely dry, and her hair is brittle.

"For a long time, I had to shave nearly every day and get my hair cut every two weeks," Wendy says. "My body was covered with fine hair called lanugo. I used to call my hairdresser and tell her, 'It's the werewolf again!'"

Lanugo is an anorexic body's way of trying to keep warm when the insulation that body fat usually provides is unavailable. Wendy's lanugo gradually disappeared as she regained weight.

Wendy feels she's been luckier than some. "One of the patients on my unit got down to thirty-five pounds and had four heart attacks," Wendy says. "She appeared on the Phil Donahue show once in a segment on eating disorders."

Not all cases of anorexia nervosa are as serious or as long-lasting as Wendy's, of course. When caught in its earliest stages, anorexia can be stopped and the recovery process started in as little as four months. That's why it's so important to recognize the warning signs of anorexia in a friend or family member and then to ask a person in authority to intervene.

3 "B" Is For Bulimia

Linda can remember the first moment she saw Justin. And she now believes that may have been the same moment her bulimia really began.

"I walked down the hall on the first day of school, my sophomore year, looking for my assigned locker," Linda recalls. "And there was Justin, a transfer student whose locker was just a few away from mine. I never believed in love at first sight until then."

Justin was friendly and funny, but obviously not as interested in Linda as she was in him. Linda says she began watching closely to see what made Justin so interested in some of the other girls. It wasn't long before she realized what they had in common.

"They were the very slim girls, what my mom would call willowy," Linda says. "I wasn't that overweight. I realize that now, but at the time, just knowing he preferred very slender women made me feel fatter."

Linda says she tried dieting. She even tried skipping meals.

"But my mother was too good a cook," Linda says, laughing. Then, more seriously, she adds, "And she kept too close an eye on my two brothers, my sister, and me. Oh, I could skip lunch, but then I'd come home starved and eat like crazy. I guess I wasn't cut out to be an anorexic—thank goodness."

In October of her sophomore year, Linda missed a week of school because of an unusually severe bout with influenza. The morning she dressed to go back to school, her clothes felt loose. Stepping on the scale, Linda discovered she'd lost twelve pounds.

"I was so happy and felt so light, I think I floated all the way to school," Linda says. "But there was one thing I remember thinking: If Justin liked my new figure enough to look at me the way he looked at those other girls, there was nothing I wouldn't do to keep it. And the more I thought about it, the more I believed there was a very simple way to do just that: the same thing that caused me to lose the weight in the first place."

It didn't take Linda long to work out the basis of what would become a classic case of bulimia nervosa. Since there was no easy way for her to rid herself of meals she ate at home, she began eating low-fat foods, such as plain cereal, skim milk, low-fat yogurt, unbuttered toast or plain bagels, or just a piece of fruit.

"I ate in the school cafeteria, just as I always had," Linda says. "Justin was paying a lot of attention to me, often joining me for lunch, and I wanted everything to look normal. Besides, my sister would rat me out to Mom if I didn't eat."

Immediately after lunch, Linda says, she would excuse herself to "comb her hair." Then she'd hurry to the nearest bathroom. Once there, she would comb her hair in front of the mirror and wait until no one else was around. When she was alone, she would enter a cubicle, stick her finger down her throat, and force herself to vomit.

"What was really strange is that I started eating more and more when people were watching," Linda says. "I'd eat two sandwiches, potato chips, candy bars, ice cream, lots of stuff for lunch. It was like I couldn't get enough to eat, but then I'd get rid of it as fast as possible. Sometimes, especially at home, I'd eat so much my stomach would hurt."

At home, Linda would use homework or reading a library book as an excuse to go directly upstairs to her room after supper. She would go into the bathroom before anyone else in her family came upstairs. She would lock the door and turn on the faucet in the sink. Then she'd repeat her after-lunch routine, wash her mouth out thoroughly, and vigorously brush her teeth. By the time her sister and brothers came upstairs, she'd be hard at work at her desk or curled up under the covers with a book.

"This is going to sound really gross, but one of the first things I learned was to throw up as soon as possible after eating so it wouldn't taste too bad," Linda says. "Another thing that made my routine seem like a good idea was the major improvement in my grades. How could they not improve? I was spending more time than ever before with my homework because it was my reason for being upstairs alone."

But two different factors really influenced Linda

to continue her bulimic behavior: one, her relationship with Justin was going really well; and two, vomiting made her feel light, heady, and pure, as if she had purged herself of something evil.

"I don't know how to describe it. I think it might be similar to what athletes call 'runner's high,'" Linda says. "But as positive as that sounds, the truth was I lived in terror. I usually got on the scale three or four times a day. If my day was going badly, or if I hadn't been able to vomit when or as much as I wanted, I'd be on a scale half a dozen times or more that day. That constant anxiety was awful." It seemed as if all she ever thought about was Justin and food.

As if the stress of bulimia wasn't enough, Linda began exercising as hard and as often as she could to help keep her weight down. She added laxatives to her routine to make up for the times she was unable to slip away into a bathroom and vomit.

Linda's relationship with Justin continued to go well until near the end of the school year. Then, Linda says, several things happened at once. "Justin's interest began to wander. I caught him holding hands with another girl, and he started making excuses for not being with me," Linda says. "My heart was breaking. I didn't know if he was bored or if I was driving him away. I didn't seem to have any energy, and I was having trouble focusing on conversations and classes."

She didn't look good or feel good, either. She was beginning to develop broken blood vessels in her eyes, and her saliva glands swelled. There were puffy areas below the corners of her mouth, and her face broke out in rashes and pimples more than normal. Worse, those grades she had raised early in the school year began to drop because she was having trouble concentrating. Often her thinking was confused and slow.

At the same time that Justin started drifting away, Linda adds, her mother began paying closer attention to her health. "What I didn't realize, maybe because I really didn't look at myself objectively, is that I had developed lines around my mouth from vomiting," Linda says. "My throat was always sore, and sometimes when I vomited it bled. I seemed to have a lot more hair on my body, especially my face."

Linda says she felt cold much of the time and had gotten into the habit of wearing a sweater constantly, even in class. But whenever her mother suggested she see their family doctor, Linda always found a reason not to make an appointment.

"The person who finally discovered what I was doing was, believe it or not, my dentist," Linda explains. "I had no idea that repeated vomiting would ruin my teeth." Linda says her dentist became alarmed when comparisons of her dental records from a year earlier showed rapid deterioration in the condition of her teeth and the beginning of gum disease.

"He called Mom in and told her to take me to a doctor immediately," Linda says. "He really scared both of us. We went directly to the doctor, and Mom went in with me. By the time the doctor finished asking questions and demanding honest answers, both he and Mom knew about my bulimia. Besides, I was tired of keeping secrets from my family and trying to handle it alone."

Linda's family doctor recommended an eating

disorder specialist at a local clinic. She began going to appointments several times each week after school. Linda's mother and father went with her, sometimes together and sometimes separately.

"The hardest thing I ever had to do was sit down with my entire family in the psychiatrist's office and tell them about my bulimia," Linda recalls. "I was so afraid they would make fun of me or call me stupid. They were stunned at first. I could see they didn't know what to say. My sister just sat there, looking at me with her eyes wide. My two older brothers couldn't seem to look at me at all."

But slowly, as the psychiatrist encouraged them all to share their feelings with Linda, she made a wonderful discovery. "As they recovered enough to start asking questions, I could see they were just as scared as I was," Linda says. "Somehow, that really helped. And it's a good thing they were so support-ive, because for the next six months I needed all the love and understanding they could give."

Linda's relationship with Justin ended, and the struggle to overcome her bulimic behavior patterns was at its roughest. She became severely depressed. "I thought I was happy all those months," Linda says. "When I really began to realize how miserable I'd actually been all that time, and what I'd been putting myself through for nothing, I felt hopeless. Worse, for a long time, I couldn't think of any way that I'd ever feel better about myself and the future."

Her home routines changed completely, Linda says. She did her homework at the dining room table near the rest of the family. In fact, Linda adds, she was never left completely alone. One or more of her siblings was always there.

"I almost couldn't take a shower alone," Linda says, chuckling. "It wasn't funny then, let me tell you. A lot of the time I wanted to be alone. And when my kid sister began hanging out with me at school during lunch break, I really got upset."

"When I told her to go back with her friends, she refused. She told me her friends understood," Linda says. "I really blew up then. I thought she'd told everyone in school about my bulimia. But she hadn't. Instead, she told her friends I was having a hard time getting over Justin. 'That's better?' I remember yelling at her. But I didn't scare her away, not at all. Bless her, she stuck through all the bitterness and anger."

Through the summer and into her junior year, Linda continued outpatient treatment at the clinic. Gradually, her compulsion to keep her weight down with bulimic behavior faded. And she gained back ten of the twelve pounds she'd so desperately tried to keep off.

"At first, I fretted about that quite a bit," Linda admits. "I had to fight with myself to stay off the scale, to eat sensibly, to tell myself that I look and feel better at the weight I was supposed to maintain. But it was never easy."

Today, Linda is a confident young woman who has graduated from high school and is ready to start college.

"Looking back on all those months I used bulimia to control my weight, I still can't believe that I went through all that because I was trying to be someone I'm not," Linda says. "One of the things I've learned is that if people don't like you for who you really are, they don't truly like you at all."

Most of all, Linda believes, you have to love yourself first.

Her relationship with Justin may have been the trigger for Linda's bulimia, but all of the underlying causes were already in place. Poor self-image, low self-esteem, lack of self-confidence, and the desire to be perfect in the eyes of a person who meant a lot to her were all powerful influences that pushed Linda toward bulimia.

Recovery from bulimia focused on more than just improving Linda's physical health and moving away from bulimic behavior.

"I talked to my psychologist about what I see when I look in the mirror, how I perceive myself in relation to those around me, and what my goals and dreams were," Linda said. "After we got done rooting around, and the dust settled, I learned a great deal about myself that I had never understood before."

Although Linda keeps in touch with her doctor, the length of time between calls is getting longer. And as Linda becomes stronger, the chance she'll go back to using bulimia to control her weight becomes smaller.

WATCH FOR THE WARNING SIGNS OF BULIMIA

You might be surprised to learn that it's easier to recognize the signs of bulimia than anorexia. As a rule, those with bulimic behavior look more ill than do anorexic patients. It's a good idea to know and understand the symptoms and behavior patterns of bulimia, so that if someone you know begins to behave differently, you'll know what it means and will be able to find help for that person. The symptoms of bulimia nervosa include:

⊙ Frequent complaints about feeling dizzy, light-headed, or faint.

⊙ Bruised or callused knuckles and fingers from sticking fingers down the throat to induce vomiting. Bulimics' faces may appear puffy, making them look fatter than usual. They may complain of sore throats, sore and swollen glands in the neck, and eye problems.

⊙ Dry skin, brittle hair, and marked hair loss. Oddly, the opposite is also true in that bulimic behavior often causes lanugo—fine hair on the face, back and arms—to grow.

⊙ Dental problems, including deterioration of both the teeth and gums.

⊙ Frequent headaches, and complaints of being cold.

⊙ Low potassium and other vitamin deficiencies can cause tingling in the hands, feet, and face; irregular or slow heartbeat is another symptom of bulimia.

⊙ Long-term effects may include loss of tooth enamel, arthritis, osteoporosis, back and joint pain, poor circulation, heart problems, sleep problems, and fatigue.

The danger signs of bulimic behavior are:

⊙ Bingeing or eating uncontrollably. You'll notice that a bulimic eats much more than usual and often eats foods he or she would not normally eat.

⊙ Purging by strict dieting, fasting, vigorous exercise, vomiting, or abusing laxatives and diuretics in an attempt to lose weight.

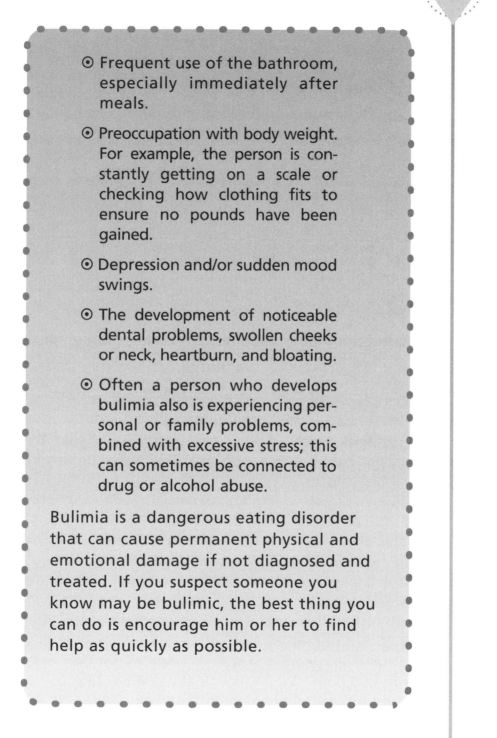

⊙ Frequent use of the bathroom, especially immediately after meals.

⊙ Preoccupation with body weight. For example, the person is constantly getting on a scale or checking how clothing fits to ensure no pounds have been gained.

⊙ Depression and/or sudden mood swings.

⊙ The development of noticeable dental problems, swollen cheeks or neck, heartburn, and bloating.

⊙ Often a person who develops bulimia also is experiencing personal or family problems, combined with excessive stress; this can sometimes be connected to drug or alcohol abuse.

Bulimia is a dangerous eating disorder that can cause permanent physical and emotional damage if not diagnosed and treated. If you suspect someone you know may be bulimic, the best thing you can do is encourage him or her to find help as quickly as possible.

4 "C" Is for Compulsive Overeating

Randy weighed more than 400 pounds when a friend convinced him to join Overeaters Anonymous.

"I didn't start out that way, of course," Randy says. "No one starts life with an eating disorder. Instead, this crept up on me like some monstrous ghost and haunted me for years."

Randy was an only child who says that he adored his parents. His mother was overweight, and as he grew up, Randy says he began to catch her doing things he didn't understand, such as hiding food and eating when she thought no one noticed. This was odd, but it wasn't something that concerned Randy until his father began to drift away.

"It wasn't like a big blowup, or arguments all the time," Randy says. "I can see clearly now, as an adult, how he simply gave up on his relationship with my mother. As a child, I didn't realize what this distancing meant and wasn't prepared for the natural outcome. When he finally asked her for a divorce, I felt all the pain in the world."

Without his father there, Randy says the center of his world and the security he felt in his family slowly faded away, too. Shaken, believing he was somehow responsible for his parents' failures, Randy began copying his mother's habits of hiding food away. When she was at work and he was home alone, Randy began to eat enormous amounts of food.

"That only made matters worse," Randy notes. "I hadn't been all that popular at school. I was shy and a serious student. Add being fat to that, and you can see why I turned to eating more and more in an effort to compensate for what I felt I was missing . . . my father, and in a different way, my mother, too."

Randy graduated from high school with honors despite his personal difficulties. Away from home for the first time, he dove into college dorm life with tremendous appetite.

"I ate. I kept the little boxy dorm refrigerator full of goodies," Randy explains. "Boxes of chocolates, jars of peanut butter, cookies, Twinkies, sodas. The little storage area I had was crammed with potato chips, crackers, you name it."

Randy says that at first he excused his night eating as fueling up for study sessions. But when he realized he was waking up during the night just so he could eat, he knew his eating habits were totally out of control.

"Nearly all I thought about, aside from studying, was food," Randy says. "I knew where the best chocolate chip cookies, lemon meringue pie, pizza, hamburgers, and cakes could be found in town. I'd tell myself I needed to go to a certain store to pick up something normal, such as bread or yogurt. But I knew, deep inside, that I'd also buy a half-gallon of ice cream, or that layer cake the store was famous for, with the best frosting in the state."

Randy says he couldn't seem to stop overeating even though he knew how destructive his eating was. Worse, it didn't make up for losing his father, nor for being laughed at or ignored by his professors and friends. Worst of all, the women on campus never gave him a second look.

All of that misery simply sent him back to the store for more food to ease the pain and low self-esteem he felt. Meanwhile, his weight rose danger-ously, to the point where it threatened his health.

"One day, I was sitting on a bench watching the world go by and eating a big candy bar when a stu-dent I recognized from my dorm complex sat down beside me," Randy says. "He sat there for a while, then asked, 'Why are you eating yourself to death?'"

Stunned, Randy says he couldn't think of any-thing to say. Then without warning, Randy burst into tears. Embarrassed, he tried to get up and walk away.

"The student put his hand on my arm, stopping me, and he said, 'I understand because I've been there,'" Randy says. "I sat back down and I listened as he told me how he overcame something he called compulsive overeating disorder with the help of an organization called Overeaters Anonymous."

"He offered to take me to a meeting," Randy says. "He told me he'd been a member for three years at that point. I couldn't believe it at first, because he was a nice-looking person of average size and build. But when he began talking about the way he used to eat, things that I was doing and thought no one else knew about, I realized I might have found a solution to what had become an unbearable situation."

Still, Randy hesitated. He told the friendly student, "I'll think about it seriously."

And he kept his promise. But going to an Overeaters Anonymous (OA) meeting represented a giant step into the unknown. Randy admits he wasn't ready to attend meetings regularly and follow the OA program . . . not yet. It took another student with a more subtle approach to convince him that the group approach to overcoming compulsive overeating might work for him.

Randy eventually joined Overeaters Anonymous with his newfound friends serving as mentors. His weight is down from more than 400 pounds to 245. It's still more than Randy says he wants to weigh ideally, but it's a world away from the secretive, painful existence he knew before he became an Overeaters Anonymous member.

"There's no miracle cure for compulsive overeating," Randy says. "I go to OA meetings every week. I share my story with those just beginning to learn what this ugly disorder is all about. And when I pass a store that I know has the best cookies or frosting in the world, I use the discipline I've learned to keep on going without going inside."

PHYSICAL SYMPTOMS OF COMPULSIVE OVEREATING

As you might guess, the body's reaction to continual overeating is the opposite of what happens in anorexic or bulimic eating disorders. Plus, there are other discomforts and bodily changes that take place when a person constantly overeats and weighs too much to be healthy.

- ⊙ Compulsive overeaters tend to be warm or hot much of the time, because they exert themselves more than people of average weight during any activity, even standing up.

- ⊙ They have fast or irregular heart rates, high blood pressure, hormone imbalances, and possible raised cholesterol levels. These conditions are common in overweight people and are often related to serious heart disease.

- ⊙ Compulsive overeaters suffer from joint pain and poor circulation caused by the additional stress placed on the body by excess weight, along with constricting of the veins and arteries.

- ⊙ They also are frequently exhausted and weak, with decreased endurance and dizziness. This is brought on by stress, nutritional imbalances, fast heart rate and high blood pressure. In general, the increased exertion caused by excess weight and increased digestive activity places greater pressure on the compulsive overeater's body.

- ⊙ They suffer from varicose and spider veins—veins that are raised from the skin, especially on the legs, and can be painful—as well as muscle soreness and decreased mobility.

EVEN SIMPLE BINGE EATING CAN BE DANGEROUS

Everyone overeats occasionally. Around the holidays or on vacation, when there are so many good things to eat, you know how easy it is to eat too much. You wind up with a stomachache and an urge to take a long nap.

That kind of bingeing isn't harmful if it doesn't become a habit. But when a person has eaten sparingly for a long time and then eats a huge amount of food in a short period of time, a binge can even be fatal.

An extreme case in London, England, involved a model who had starved herself down to eighty-four pounds, then went on a binge. According to an account in the British medical journal *Lancet,* the woman ate so much that she gained nineteen pounds in an extremely short time. As far as doctors could discover, she had eaten liver, kidneys, steaks, eggs, cheese, bread, mushrooms, carrots, a whole cauliflower, ten peaches, four pears, two apples, four bananas, two pounds of plums, two pounds of grapes, and two glasses of milk, all in a single day. After eating all this, she died. Others have required hospitalization because their stomachs have split open, unable to hold the sudden input of too much food.

Such extremes may be rare, but for compulsive overeaters, the urge to binge becomes constant and powerful. The anxiety beneath the compulsion to eat in such an unhealthy manner, and the inability to stop eating when the person knows he or she has gone far beyond what is healthy, is difficult to understand. It takes the objectivity and professional knowledge of eating disorder experts to help unravel the puzzle of why a person would do something that causes pain and potential physical damage.

BINGE EATING DANGER SIGNALS

Some experts estimate that up to 40 percent of overweight people may be binge eaters. In addition to depression and other psychological problems, these are the trouble signs to watch for:

⊙ Episodes of binge eating. Even though binge eaters tend to do this secretly, it's possible you might see them eating more at one time than appears healthy.

⊙ Eating when not physically hungry. Binge eaters eat at any time, day or night, sometimes soon after a heavy meal. The need to continue eating has little to do with hunger. Instead, they are trying to feed, or soothe, a different kind of need.

⊙ Frequent dieting. Oddly, binge eaters and compulsive overeaters are often on diets, at least publicly. They may talk about food a lot and spend time working on menus.

⊙ Feeling unable to stop eating voluntarily. When most people are full and ready to stop, compulsive overeaters continue to eat, consuming huge amounts of food.

⊙ Awareness that their eating patterns are abnormal. Compulsive overeaters will admit to eating too much at a time consistently, but they may also tell you that they just can't help themselves.

⊙ Constant weight fluctuations. Compulsive overeaters lose and gain weight constantly; this pattern is sometimes called "yo-yo" dieting. Typically, the compulsive overeater is able to diet successfully for a short period of time and lose weight. Suddenly, however, you will notice that he or she has gained back the weight, and usually more.

⊙ Depression. You know how you feel when you don't seem to be able to control events in your life. Binge eaters feel that way all the time.

⊙ Relating their self-esteem and success in social life or career to their weight. If a compulsive overeater fails in one of these areas, he or she is more likely to blame the fact that he or she is overweight than on another reason. If successful in these areas, he or she may tell you that successful dieting has made him or her more acceptable or effective.

COULD SOMEONE I KNOW BE A COMPULSIVE OVEREATER?

If you're concerned that someone you care about may be a compulsive overeater, try this test. For each statement, think about the person and answer "yes" or "no" depending on whether the statement applies or does not apply to that person's behavior and eating habits.

- ⊙ The person has been on more diets than you can count.
- ⊙ The person has lost and regained weight many times.
- ⊙ The person seems to think about food all the time—what to eat, when to eat, where to eat, what was just eaten, the fat, carbohydrate, and protein content of foods, and how he or she is going to avoid overeating or stay on a diet.
- ⊙ The person defines how "good" or "bad" he or she is based on what foods are eaten and how much the person weighs.
- ⊙ The person has trouble identifying real hunger and fullness; he or she feels hungry all the time.

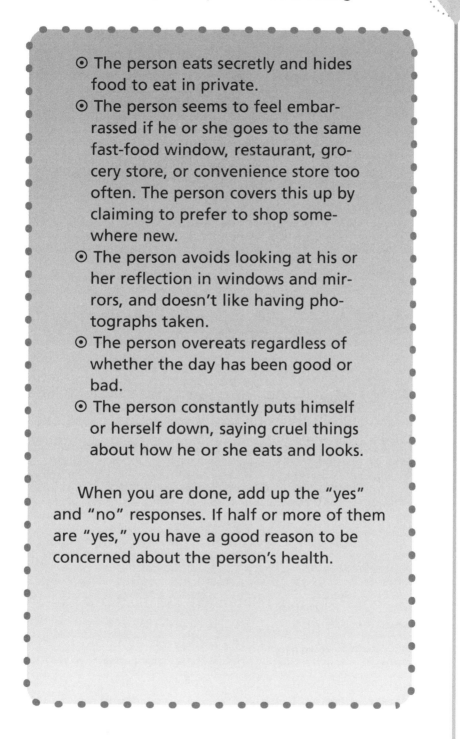

- The person eats secretly and hides food to eat in private.
- The person seems to feel embarrassed if he or she goes to the same fast-food window, restaurant, grocery store, or convenience store too often. The person covers this up by claiming to prefer to shop somewhere new.
- The person avoids looking at his or her reflection in windows and mirrors, and doesn't like having photographs taken.
- The person overeats regardless of whether the day has been good or bad.
- The person constantly puts himself or herself down, saying cruel things about how he or she eats and looks.

When you are done, add up the "yes" and "no" responses. If half or more of them are "yes," you have a good reason to be concerned about the person's health.

5 Compulsive Exercise

You've been told all your life that exercise is good for you. And that's true, up to a point. But there is a point at which exercise stops being beneficial and becomes a psychological disorder called compulsive exercise or exercise addiction.

You probably know at least one dedicated athlete, a person who exercises in a disciplined manner and maintains a fine-tuned muscular body through daily weight training or aerobic sessions. Maybe you are that type of exerciser yourself. That is a healthy way to stay in shape.

Compulsive exercisers go beyond regular workouts. They exercise to or even past the point of pain to burn calories and lose weight. Their self-esteem is directly related to how much they have exercised in a given day, and if they are unable to exercise as much as they believe they should, they become depressed. The difference between dedication and compulsion is one of balance. A dedicated athlete works through an effective, safe exercise routine with measurable goals, eats wholesome foods, and knows when to rest. On the other hand, a person with compulsive exercise disorder pushes his or her body constantly, diets rigorously, and often uses laxatives or diuretics to lose more weight.

Compulsive exercise is one of the symptoms of anorexia and bulimia, but it can also occur as a separate disorder. What happens to the person who gets caught up in its unhealthy cycle is similar to what happens to people with the other eating disorders you've read about in earlier chapters.

There are two main reasons why compulsive exercisers do what they do. First, they feel—consciously or not—an enormous need to control a lifestyle or situation that they believe is out of control. It doesn't matter what or where the trouble is . . . at school, at home with parents or siblings, at work, or in friendships or romantic relationships. The second reason is to lose weight and maintain what may be an unrealistic body image. Compulsive exercisers believe that the more they work out, the slimmer they will become. Unfortunately, that isn't always true. Too frequently, compulsive exercise is teamed with compulsive overeating. The person gets so hungry from all that exercise and stringent dieting that binge eating becomes a factor.

"It's a dangerous cycle. I know because I was caught up in it for a long time," Randy says. "I would stop at a store for a half-gallon of ice cream and a half-dozen cupcakes with lots of frosting. I'd eat all or most of it in one evening. Then I'd start feeling guilty. I'd starve myself the next day, skip breakfast and supper. Then I'd hit the gym and work out really hard for a couple of hours."

After the workout, Randy adds, he'd be so hungry he'd stop at the nearest grocery store or fast-food restaurant and overeat again. "The worst part of it was the guilt and the feeling of helplessness," Randy says. "I just didn't seem to be able to break the cycle."

For those with anorexia and bulimia, exercise addiction is a fairly common companion disorder. Because these people don't eat enough to compensate for the amount of exercise they do, they put a tremendous strain on their bodies. The combination of insufficient food and too much exercise over a prolonged period of time can permanently damage the person's internal organs and bone structure. Eventually, the person may die if the cycle of starvation and excessive exercise isn't broken.

In a February 1998 interview in *Family Circle* magazine, a young woman named Rebecca Manley talked about her struggle to overcome compulsive exercise disorder. Diagnosed with anorexia nervosa at seventeen, Rebecca seemed to have overcome her disorder by the time she started college. But the truth was that she had simply become an expert at hiding the truth. Rebecca was taking more than one hundred laxatives a day and often skipped work to exercise at a local gym for eight hours or longer.

Rebecca got into dangerously poor physical condition before she realized how serious her eating disorder was and how much it had affected her life. At the lowest point in her illness, Rebecca said, she had no friends left, had lost her job, and felt entirely alone.

With counseling, Rebecca was able to recover

from both anorexia and compulsive exercise disorder. Aware that many others needed the experience and insight into compulsive exercise she had to share, she founded the Massachusetts Eating Disorders Association in Newton, Massachusetts. You'll read more about Rebecca later.

For Linda, excessive exercise was a part of her bulimic behavior, another way to purge after a binge. "Exercise was one of the first things I used to keep off the weight I lost when I had the flu," Linda says. "I started walking, then jogging daily. I joined the cross-country team at school because I knew they went through a strenuous conditioning workout every day. It was the perfect way to hide my real goal—controlling my weight."

Linda says she often spent hours in her room running quietly in place so no one would hear. But even if they did, she had a built-in excuse for her behavior because of the cross-country team.

Wendy also admits to using exercise as a weight control method in combination with her anorexic behavior. "The office building where I worked had a one-mile walking track laid out around it," Wendy says. "I'd walk it for my morning break, then again at noon instead of eating lunch, and once more during my afternoon break. I remember wishing I had time to get out of the office even more than that."

WARNING SIGNS OF COMPULSIVE EXERCISE DISORDER

⊙ Exercising daily for hours at a time, either in a gym or at home. Compulsive exercisers are constantly pedaling on a stationary bicycle, jumping rope, or using a treadmill. They have exercise equipment in their homes or have access to a health center or gym where they spend all their free time.

⊙ Signing up for one exercise class after another, sometimes four or five at a time, at the gym or other health club.

⊙ Exercising instead of participating in social activities, work, or school. Compulsive exercisers abandon favorite pastimes, such as going to movies and shopping, in order to leave more time for exercise. They may ignore or withdraw from friends who do not share their addiction to exercise.

⊙ Constant discussion of or concern about dieting, exercise, and weight control to the exclusion of other topics.

⊙ Spending long periods of time alone and unseen. Compulsive exercisers become skilled at hiding the amount of exercise they do from family or friends.

⊙ Showing signs of eating disorders. Compulsive exercise often develops along with anorexia or bulimia, so the symptoms of those two eating disorders are also signs that the person needs help.

MUSCLE DYSMORPHIA: A NEW DISORDER

Medical professionals have recently recognized the existence of another kind of psychological disorder that they have named muscle dysmorphia.

Oddly, muscle dysmorphia appears to be the opposite of anorexia. Instead of having a self-image of being too fat or big, a person with muscle dysmorphia believes that his or her body is too small and weak, without enough muscle.

Anorexic people typically diet until they are severely underweight. Yet when they see themselves reflected in a mirror, they still believe they are too fat. In contrast, those with muscle dysmorphia work hard for hours every day to "pump themselves up." But when they look at themselves, they believe they are hopelessly out of shape and much too small.

Muscle dysmorphia occurs in men and women, as do anorexia and bulimia. Women are still most likely to be victims of anorexia and bulimia, however, and it appears that men are more likely to develop muscle dysmorphia than are women. The reasons for this tendency are unclear and may come from a deep-rooted sense of how each gender naturally perceives itself in relation to the outside world.

As with compulsive exercise disorder, those diagnosed with muscle dysmorphia willingly give up good jobs, careers, and social interaction to spend hours every day at the gym "bulking up." People with the disorder may be so self-conscious about their bodies that they refuse to go anywhere their bodies might be bared and subjected to close scrutiny. Worse, many resort to taking anabolic steroids or other performance-enhancing drugs to help them build bigger muscles. Anabolic steroids have serious physical and emotional side effects that include irrational and even violent behavior. Still, muscle dysmorphics honestly believe they are like the old advertisement about the "ninety-seven-pound weakling" on the beach who gets sand kicked in his face by the muscular bully. In fact, specialists are now talking about muscle dysmorphia as the body image disorder of the 1990s, in the same way that anorexia and bulimia were prominently discussed and debated in the 1980s.

Americans appear to be especially vulnerable to exercise compulsion and muscle dysmorphia. We spend an estimated $1 billion each year on commercial gym memberships. More than a million Americans work out at home.

"Strong dedication to bodybuilding or other sports is usually perfectly healthy," Pope says. "However, ordinary athletes do not experience the profound body dissatisfaction, severe stress, and loss of interest in social or professional activities as we have found in those with muscle dysmorphia."

HOW MUCH IS TOO MUCH?

Every person is different, so it's difficult to draw a line between how much exercise is enough and how much is too much. It's not a matter of physical need. Each human being needs exercise just as he or she requires food, air, water, and other elements for a healthy lifestyle. It comes down to finding the right amount of each to keep an individual in optimum shape. You know people who exercise more than you do, and others who exercise less. Each has a choice in how much is the right amount for him or her. Of course, there are times when you naturally exercise more than at other times. Vacations spent hiking, biking, skiing, swimming, snorkeling, or enjoying other sports can entice people into exercising more than they normally would. But when a person begins to exercise at the expense of those other essentials, there may be reason for concern.

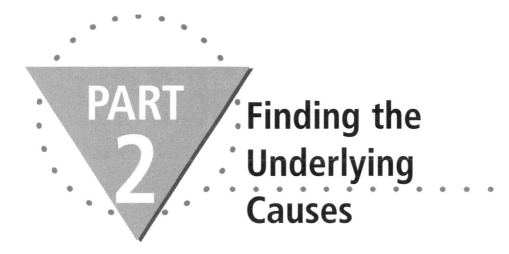

PART 2

Finding the Underlying Causes

6

When Your Worst Enemy Is You

Everyone has dreams and goals, things they want to achieve next week, next month, or even years down the road. For certain groups of people, those goals require discipline and effort far beyond what the rest of us exert. Athletes, dancers, models, performers, and public leaders all exercise tremendous control over their bodies, their time, and their lives. They demand a lot of themselves and have difficult goals they strive to reach. Somewhat surprisingly, these self-controlled, disciplined people seem to be the ones most likely to suffer from eating disorders.

It's not hard to find horror stories about people who have been unable to recover from eating disorders. World-class gymnast Christy Henrich, for example, was twenty-two years old when she died in 1994 as the result of an eating disorder. She weighed only sixty pounds at her death. Mary Wazeter was a promising long-distance runner until, depressed over her eating disorder, she jumped from a bridge in 1992 in a suicide attempt and broke her back. She will spend the rest of her life in a wheelchair. And you've already read about superstar musician and vocalist Karen Carpenter's struggle with anorexia and bulimia in the introduction to this book.

But many famous people have succeeded in overcoming eating disorders, too. They include actress Sally Field, actress and exercise guru Jane Fonda, and gymnast Cathy Rigby. One of the most visible, successful examples of a celebrity who overcame an eating disorder was Lady Diana Spencer, Princess of Wales. Diana was young and had led a sheltered life before her marriage to Prince Charles thrust her into the public eye. At the same time, she was expected to fulfill the demands of aristocracy, which included adhering to a rigid daily schedule of public appearances, and to be the mother of England's next generation of kings.

Under constant pressure to be perfect, to look beautiful and poised at all times, despite the rude behavior of photographers and reporters and a seemingly fairy-tale marriage that wasn't going to let her live happily ever after, Princess Di became bulimic. Her photographs in the world's tabloid newspapers at that time depicted a beautiful woman who was entirely too thin.

It's remarkable that Princess Di was eventually able to overcome her bulimia. The loss of privacy and the stress of her public position became even more intense as time passed. She was able not only to recover from bulimia, but to command the respect and love of people around the world, to put her unique position to work for charities, and to earn a place in history that will not be forgotten.

"Princess Di is my heroine," Wendy says. "I have photograph books of her all over my house. When I feel as though I can't go on, that the pressures of everyday life are more than I can bear, I think about Princess Di and tell myself that if she could recover from an eating disorder with all she had to face, I can maintain my recovery from anorexia."

Of course, there are also tens of thousands of ordinary people such as Wendy, Linda, and Randy who have battled and won against eating disorders. Since the early 1980s, when eating disorders were first isolated as a separate and serious psychological problem, dozens of ways to treat eating disorders have been developed.

Medical and mental health professionals have learned that no single therapy works for all eating disorder patients. Although they have specific names for the different types of disorders—anorexia, bulimia, compulsive overeating, binge-and-purge, and more—the reasons why people develop them are as individual as the people themselves. It only makes sense, therefore, that a wide variety of treatment plans are needed to help change the way these people perceive themselves and to find the way to lifelong physical and emotional health.

Despite the differences in the way people develop and experience eating disorders, these people do have certain things in common. The need to be perfect, the need to meet unreasonably high expectations, the need to feel in control of at least one aspect of life, and the need to earn the respect or admiration of one (or more) important person in their lives are some of the driving forces behind the development of eating disorders.

Meghan McDonald, a high school junior in Racine, Wisconsin, was considered one of the top swimmers in her state until a painful elbow injury prevented her from competing. After six years of practice every day with the expectation of success-fully competing in the state meet, Meghan learned that she would have to stop swimming and weight training for a whole year to allow her elbow to heal.

For someone used to working hard toward a specific goal, the inactivity was difficult to bear. Meghan became severely depressed and eventually became anorexic. Just eight days after the state meet, the young athlete entered Rogers Memorial Hospital in Oconomowoc, which specializes in the treatment of eating disorders. The five-foot, nine-inch swimmer had lost about twenty-five pounds, down from her normal 140 pounds.

The one thing that helped Meghan focus on her-self and getting well was her swimming. Her thera-pist at the hospital used her desire to get back into the water to overcome Meghan's anorexia. She urged Meghan to nourish her muscles since she would not eat for herself. The therapist used Meghan's love of swimming as a "lever" to help her see eating in a different light.

Sadly, as in Meghan's case, extreme eating dis-orders such as anorexia, bulimia, and compulsive overeating result in the opposite of perfection. An eating disorder never helps a person meet the goals set or fulfill any needs. Instead, eating disorders dis-rupt families, interrupt education, damage careers, and destroy relationships. Meghan still requires medication for depression and sees a psychiatrist every two months.

Even less severe eating disorders adversely affect people who are working toward a goal. Binge eating, fad dieting, fasting, and nutritionally inadequate liquid diets regularly rob these people of the power of concentration, leach muscles and bones of vital nutrients, and interfere with sleep.

Statistics show that eating disorders are most common among middle- to upper-class females ranging in age from twelve to twenty-five. This is, not coincidentally, a group from which much is expected: good health and attractiveness, intelligence of a degree to assure entry into college or other top career opportunities, and the financial support to achieve whatever athletic, professional or academic goals they set for themselves.

There's nothing wrong with striving to be the best you can possibly be, but that desire must be accompanied by acceptance of yourself as you are, with strengths and flaws like any human being. The trouble starts when you lose track of how to balance what you can achieve against what you cannot.

THE KEYS TO RECOVERY

If you are struggling with an eating disorder, successful recovery depends on one person: you. No magic pills or potions exist that will rid a person of an eating disorder. They can't be wished away nor surgically removed. Time won't heal this problem; it will only grow worse untreated. Your own willpower is the key to recovery from an eating disorder. No one else can recover for you, but that's also the downside of recovery. You can be your own best friend or your own worst enemy.

The decision to go forward with recovery is a tough one to make, because eating disorders become powerful tools for facing the pressures and problems we all face. A part of you will want to hold onto that tool for dear life, even when common sense tells you that the tool itself may actually end your life.

Some eating disorder specialists believe that it is very difficult for anorexic or bulimic patients to give up their behaviors because the disorder has some sort of value to them. That is why people who have committed themselves to the recovery process must meet their team of physicians, dietitians, and therapists more than halfway. Any less of an effort will probably end in failure.

Part of you doesn't want to give up the eating disorder because it has allowed you to avoid facing the real problems behind it. By focusing on a food obsession and controlling both what you eat and how much you weigh, you've found a way to get around dealing with all those impossibly high expectations and the things in your life you want to control but can't.

Some people—most commonly athletes, ballet dancers, and models—develop eating disorders because they must maintain a low body weight to be competitive. They may have been encouraged to lose weight by trainers, teachers, agents, or other people who have influence over them. These influential fig- ures do not intend to cause anyone to develop an eat- ing disorder. They simply want to help the people they are training to achieve the body type that is required in those fields. Nonetheless, the end result is often dis- ordered eating behaviors. When the need to keep weight down develops into an eating disorder, people in these demanding professions begin to lose the physical strength and mental focus that they need to achieve the goals they've set for themselves.

Others, such as Linda, become anorexic or bulimic because they believe being slim is the only way they will be accepted or loved by those they love. They literally starve themselves nearly to death trying to meet someone else's unrealistic expectations for body size and shape.

Our society has an unhealthy preoccupation with weight and body image. Still, food itself is seldom what an eating disorder is all about. The way people with eating disorders consume food, or don't do so, is the outward symptom of a wide variety of inner problems and turmoil. Eating, or not eating, is how they choose to compensate for those things they can't control or to strive for goals that are beyond their grasp.

"I wanted my father to stay with me," Randy says. "When he didn't, when he sort of faded out of my life, I turned to compulsive overeating as a way to compensate for losing him instead of facing that loss." Randy understands that it wasn't the food he really craved but a good relationship with his father. After his father was no longer available, Randy started eating more and more, trying to fill the emptiness he felt because of his father's absence. Food was always available, right there whenever he needed it. And because it was his mother's way of dealing with reality as well, Randy equated all that food with comfort and security even more.

"Then there was guilt," Randy adds. "I felt that, for some reason, I had failed my father and that's why he left us. I thought it must have been my fault, that I didn't live up to his expectations, didn't have his respect and love, things I desperately wanted. I transferred all that guilt onto the binge-eating behavior I developed."

FINDING SUPPORT

Although recovery can only begin when a person who has developed an eating disorder accepts that situation and decides to change, he or she can't do it alone. Identifying and confronting the root causes of an eating disorder is a difficult and painful process, and people with eating disorders do not have to face this process without help.

Medical care and counseling, self-help groups such as Overeaters Anonymous, and people who care about what happens to them are all important elements of the recovery process for people with eating disorders. They need professional counseling and treatment in a positive environment. The support, cooperation and understanding of family, friends, coworkers, and employers is also vital to successful recovery.

When things threaten to get out of balance now, Randy has a buddy from Overeaters Anonymous he can call and talk to about his feelings. Randy returns the favor when his buddy is feeling the pressure and pain of his compulsion to overeat. "We just take it one day at a time," Randy says. "One day is not so overwhelming that we can't handle it with a little help from a friend."

Linda also knows what it means to take the recovery process step-by-step. "I don't know what would have happened to me if I hadn't had my family and friends to lean on during my recovery from bulimia," Linda says. "When my boyfriend betrayed me, you'd think I would have stopped that behavior pattern on my own. But I know now it probably would only have gotten worse. I'm afraid to think of where I'd be today if not for the patience and understanding of everyone around me."

7 Image Is Everything?

In the classic fairy tale "Snow White," the wicked stepmother owned a magic mirror that told her she was the fairest of them all.

But one day Snow White was reflected in the magic mirror. After that, because mirrors cannot lie but only reflect a true image, the mirror told the wicked stepmother that Snow White was fairer. As in the fairy tale, in reality there are people who look into the mirror and do not see themselves clearly at all.

When we look at ourselves, what we see may differ from how others see us, and even from the truth. That perception might also mirror one or more of the separate but equally vital aspects of how we see ourselves. Self-image, body image, and self-esteem are important in relation to how we see ourselves compared to the rest of the world.

While these three aspects of self are closely aligned, the term "body image" refers to how we see our bodies literally, our physical selves. "Self-image" adds the dimension of how we think of ourselves, both physically and mentally, including our personalities as well as physical traits. "Self-esteem" refers more to how we feel about ourselves, our accomplishments, talents, and possibilities.

Like the crazy mirrors you find in carnival attractions that distort your image, making you look taller, shorter, wider, or narrower, the mind can play tricks on you and make you believe you look different from the way you really do. It's not unusual for those with eating disorders to have a mildly to severely distorted view of themselves. And when they compare their body or personality to others, they are very critical of themselves. They look at another person and wish they could be as slim, funny, smart, successful, or happy as that person seems to be. They are also affected, as most of us are, by the images of thin, happy people that are constantly presented to us in the media.

But the reality is that people with eating disorders can't seem to see their own good points because of low self-esteem. They don't value themselves as much as they value those around them.

"The very first thing that happened to trigger my anorexia was that my parents didn't believe me when I said I had been abused by a relative," Wendy says. "What I thought is that I must not be worth as much to them as that other person, since they believed him and not me. Even at an early age, I believed I wasn't as good as everybody else."

Wendy says low self-esteem was the main cause of her anorexia, but she didn't realize that until many years into therapy. It took a long time for Wendy to accept that she was equal in value to anyone else.

"I felt I didn't deserve to eat, that food was

wasted on me," Wendy added. "That feeling led to depression, and the belief that I wasn't as smart or as attractive as anyone else. Along with low self-esteem, I developed the urgent need to feel in control of at least one thing in my life." That one area, Wendy explains, was how much and when she ate. Eating, or not eating, along with the concern it caused her parents, was one of the weapons Wendy says she used to get even with her parents for not caring enough to protect her from an abuser.

As the years passed, the belief that she was not as good as everyone else became so much a part of Wendy's personality that it took years and a lot of hard work to convince herself she deserved to be well-fed and comfortable.

Often, men and women with eating disorders personalize the actions of those around them and think that everything a person or company says or does is aimed directly at them. They see compliments as just empty, polite gestures, because seen through the eyes of low self-esteem, they couldn't possibly be true.

"I remember that every time someone told me I looked especially nice, or I had done a good job on an assignment, I would tell them how stupid or ugly I really was," Wendy says. "Or, I'd immediately describe something that happened to me that made me look bad. I just couldn't accept that another person believed I was special."

SELF-IMAGE: REAL VS. IDEAL

Poor body image is another major part of eating disorders. At the beginning of the twentieth century, women especially were thought to be beautiful when they were slightly plump. A rounded figure was much to be desired. But that has changed over the course of the century, most obviously in the 1960s, when Twiggy and other models like her became extremely popular. Twiggy was an extremely slim English model whose popularity thrust the idea that "thin is in" into the world spotlight. Seemingly overnight, the image of the ideal woman changed completely. Fashion magazines began to show clothing on pencil-thin models, and women all over the world tried to copy that image. But not everyone is meant to be slim, nor to fit any one single image. The desire to match an unrealistic body image can become so great it triggers an eating disorder.

"When it became obvious that the man I thought I loved preferred very slim women, I desperately wanted to lose weight even though there really wasn't anything wrong with how I looked before," Linda explains.

Linda says when she looked in her mirror, she saw a fat person looking back at her.

"I'd study my upper arms, which I thought were flabby," Linda says. "Then I'd examine my legs and berate myself because they were too fat. I believed I had rolls of fat around my waist and clumped at my hips. I was so disgusted with myself, it would make me sick to my stomach. So I'd go to the bathroom and try to throw up again."

"It's as if we don't see ourselves, not really," Randy says. "As I continued to gain weight and binge-eat, I constantly compared myself to others and decided I wasn't as fat as they were. I guess I believed that being able to point out others who I felt looked worse made my overweight and compulsive eating disorder less of a problem."

Nothing could have been further from the truth, Randy admits. But even stranger, he says, was that when he looked in a mirror, he never really saw how much he had gained nor just how wide he was. When he had to buy clothing in steadily increasing sizes, Randy says he blamed the manufacturers for skimping on the fabric and sizes.

"I found I could mentally lie to myself about everything, including my body image. Believe it or not, it was easy," Randy says. "It was hard to face all that fat and acknowledge its existence. But reality checks are a necessary part of recovering from an eating disorder. We all had to learn to see the truth."

THE NEED FOR PERFECTION

One of the signs of an eating disorder is black-and-white thinking. With this type of extreme thinking, negative situations or feelings are equal to having the whole world come to an end, while positive situations are like having Christmas every day. People who think this way don't recognize that there is a middle ground. They expect and demand perfection in themselves, and since perfection is impossible to achieve, they often end up considering themselves failures.

This way of looking at the world triggers irrational behavior, with harsh mood swings from one extreme to the other. Linda demonstrated this with her single-minded need to keep off the weight she lost, no matter what the cost. "I let nothing get in the way of my bulimic routine," Linda says. "I had to stick to the regimen so I wouldn't gain another ounce. If I didn't, if I failed to do exactly what I had decided I needed to do to keep the weight off, I was afraid I'd gain weight."

Linda says she'd feel frantic and threatened if anyone or anything changed her schedule, and she'd feel like a failure if she did not meet her own expectations of the right behavior.

That need became a drive for perfection, not only in her efforts to keep weight off but in other areas as well. Linda felt the urge to be totally in control of how she appeared to Justin and everyone else. "My grades had to be perfect," Linda says. "So did my hair, my nails, my clothes. Looking back now, I still can't believe how miserable I was. But at the time, I believed I was happy because I was keeping my boyfriend happy."

People with eating disorders also tend to take on responsibility for things beyond their control. They want to change the world, or make others feel healthier and happier. They want to take control, not only of their own lives, but others' as well. When they fail to achieve those goals, they punish themselves with hurtful words or actions.

"I wanted my father to stay with us," Randy says. "And I wanted my mother and father to live happily ever after, just as if their marriage was a fairy tale. Of course, I understand now how unrealistic that was. I've accepted the idea that I wasn't responsible for their marriage breaking up, nor did I ever have the power to change the way they felt about each other."

Self-blame and negative thinking are still more

behavioral traits that are connected to the development of eating disorders. In turn, some blame others for their illness. "I recall thinking over and over that if my parents had only believed me about the abusive situation and had supported me, I wouldn't have gotten sick," Wendy explained.

As you can see from what Wendy, Linda, and Randy have to say about their eating disorders, food, and how they used it, was at the center of how they reacted to the world around them. But eating or not eating was only the outward sign of a lot of inner turmoil.

For those with anorexia or bulimia, not eating is a way of controlling a world they feel is out of control. For compulsive overeaters, eating is a way to avoid dealing with how they feel. They use food to help cope with stress, to take away the pain in their lives and to give them comfort.

"I realized I ate to gain weight so I could avoid close relationships and feeling vulnerable," Randy says. "My being overweight kept others from getting close, so I wouldn't have to worry about losing someone I loved again, as I did my father."

Eating or not eating is a negative way to cope with reality and unpleasant emotions. But eating disorders are really all about unresolved emotional conflicts and not about food at all. This means that coaxing a person with anorexia to eat something won't solve the problem. Nor will telling a person with bulimia to stay away from the bathroom or putting a binge eater or compulsive overeater on a diet. Any attempt to change the outward symptoms of an eating disorder without addressing the underlying problems is doomed to failure. That's why it's important for a person who has developed an eating disorder to seek professional help. Unless people with eating disorders find the right professional therapist to explain why they feel the way they do and help them work through their problems and misconceptions, no treatment will be long-lasting.

That is also why you should try to find help for a family member or friend if you suspect that person has an eating disorder. Eating disorders are outward signs of deep psychological problems within. You cannot make someone with an eating disorder seek help, but you can assist them in finding help when they are ready. Then you can offer your support and be there for the person as he or she recovers.

8 Influential Relationships

Although one person may have the eating disorder, many people directly related to or involved in behavior may have some effect on either its onset or the recovery process.

Mothers and fathers are our first role models. Even animals learn behaviors from their parents, such as where to find food and water in their immediate area and what to fear.

Humans draw vital information about who they are and how they should behave through contact with other humans from the day of their birth. This information comes first and perhaps most powerfully from parents, then from siblings, friends, teachers, romantic partners, coaches, colleagues, bosses, and others who become important in their lives. The influences these key people exert can be positive or negative.

The influence a strong, positive role model might have on you could turn out to be two-sided. Following the lead of an inspirational or extremely talented person could raise your ambitions and capabilities accordingly. On the other hand, trying to live up to someone's high-achieving example and falling short could badly damage an already fragile self-image.

In the same way, negative influences can cut both ways. You might look at someone whom you feel is a poor role model and decide not to be like them. But you might just believe that person is having more fun than you are and copy them. That's how many people get involved in substance abuse and criminal behavior.

Each person is ultimately responsible for his or her own behavior, but the influence of others plays an important role in the person's choosing that behavior. When it comes to the development and recovery processes of an eating disorder, the power of those who are closest to the victim can never be overestimated.

"The negative influence my boyfriend Justin had on my developing bulimia is obvious to me now," Linda says. "Not that I can honestly blame him. At the beginning of my recovery therapy, I really believed he was the one at fault, because the only way I thought I could please him was to stay thin. That meant doing whatever it took to keep the weight off."

Linda explains that at first, when her bulimia was diagnosed, she blamed her former boyfriend, her friends, and her family for her eating disorder. "Trying to maintain a relationship based on something I was never meant to be—extremely thin—was what I chose to do," Linda says. "I didn't want to be accountable for the choices I willingly made. It took talking about my misconceptions with a therapist for a long time before I accepted responsibility for the leading role I played in my eating disorder." Linda says she also blamed her parents and siblings for not recognizing that something was wrong with her behavior at home. Yet even now, she admits it probably wouldn't have done any good.

"I felt the same about my close friends," Linda says. "I couldn't believe they didn't notice how different I was acting. Part of me wanted them to notice and do something about it. Another part was terrified they would find out and do something to make me stop. I was a mess, emotionally and physically."

Sick, miserable, and depressed, Linda says she was secretly relieved when the dentist insisted that her mother take her to see a doctor. "That's when I really found out who my friends were," Linda added. "I expected my brothers to tell me how stupid I was acting, but they didn't. I was amazed and grateful. They were concerned, protective, and supportive. So was my kid sister, who usually was a real pain. The whole family rallied around me."

Linda says part of her therapy included being honest with her friends about her eating disorder. This was essential for two reasons. First, Linda needed to accept accountability not just at home but in school and elsewhere, and second, because the more people who knew, the less chance she had of regressing to her bulimic patterns.

"A couple of girls I considered friends blew me off after I broke up with my boyfriend and began therapy," Linda says. "I realize now they never were true friends. I'm not sure, but I think they just liked me because I was popular and dating a cool guy. That's no basis for a good friendship."

Linda says she understands how vulnerable she was to the criticism and impossible ideals of another. "Now, when I finally find that one man who will be my partner for life, I want to know, more than anything else, that he will love me for who I am," Linda says. "I'm never going to try to fit someone's image of perfection again."

Randy says he had the exact opposite problems with friends and food. "I ate in place of having friends," Randy says. "I ate instead of going out on dates. I understand now that I did that because I was afraid of close relationships. My father hurt me by leaving the family. My mother had the same problem I developed. She was a binge eater, and so was I. Staying fat put a nice, soft cushion between me and people."

Randy's compulsive overeating disorder started when he was very young. Some of his feelings, including low self-esteem, evolved directly from his disintegrating relationship with his parents. Nothing happened between early childhood and the years he spent growing up to challenge the poor image he had of himself and his value.

It took a very special friendship with a woman we'll call Mary to change Randy's life. "One semester, Mary attended two of the same classes at college that I did," Randy says. "That was when I'd almost hit my all-time worst weight . . . 403 pounds. We started by nodding to each other as we went in and out of class. I noticed Mary because she noticed me and deliberately made eye contact. No one else paid any attention to me at all."

Randy says the friendship between him and Mary started very slowly, with a nod or a little wave, and then an occasional "hello." They began to run into each other in the hallway on the way to one class or another. But, Randy says, it was nearly a month before they actually had a conversation that went past "hello" and the weather.

"I realize now that she knew how shy I was," Randy explained. "That's because she'd been there before. But of course, I didn't know that until several months later."

One rainy afternoon, when Randy and Mary were sipping coffee in a campus cafeteria, Mary calmly told Randy that she had once weighed more than 300 pounds. Sitting there, looking at Mary, who was maybe a bit chubby but nowhere near fat, Randy says he was stunned.

"Mary took a huge risk to help me by telling me about her own weight problem. I could have gotten up and walked away," Randy says. "She told me a woman friend had introduced her to Overeaters Anonymous three years before, when Mary had just graduated from high school. Mary told me the entire story, and then she looked me straight in the eyes and added, 'I like you a lot, Randy. I consider you a friend, and I don't want to see you die young.'"

Randy says he took a few days to think it over. He had tried OA once without success. But he decided that he was now ready to make a serious effort to change his behavior. He called Mary to ask if he could go to an OA meeting with her. She agreed.

"I'm afraid to think where I'd be today if it hadn't been for Mary and the chance she took to help me," Randy says. "Now I have all the support I need and a lot of friends who know exactly what I've overcome. It's made a world of difference in my life."

Wendy says she didn't have her parents' support when she needed it most, and now that they are supportive of her recovery efforts, it's probably too late.

"They knew I had a problem by the time I was five or six years old, but they didn't know what to do about it, so they yelled at me to eat," Wendy says. "I don't remember any of my grade school teachers saying or doing anything about my extreme thinness. If they did mention it to my parents, nothing was ever done about it when I was present."

Wendy adds that she felt very isolated and lonely most of her childhood. "I don't know what my classmates thought about me in school, but by junior high they must have known I had an eating problem," Wendy says. "I often had the feeling that a few of my classmates actually envied my slimness. Little did they know."

Wendy says she still fights with her father, especially when he tries to run her life. "At thirty-four, you wouldn't think I'd still have to face this problem," Wendy says. "I was Daddy's perfectly wonderful little girl, and he still sees me that way. My real friends are the people with whom I work every day." Wendy says several of her co-workers remained supportive and caring, even traveling nearly 200 miles on a regular basis to visit her while she was hospitalized for months. They'd take her out to eat and go shopping, Wendy says. And they wrote frequently, sending funny cards and thoughtful little gifts.

"Now that I'm back at work, they still look out for me all the time, and make sure I don't skimp on lunch," Wendy says, laughing. "They don't cut me any slack about having a good lunch, not just a few bites of lettuce and a diet soda like I used to eat."

Dominating parents such as Wendy's and Randy's frequently are part of an eating disorder pattern. Karen Carpenter had a similar relationship with her mother. Once, a fan complained to Karen and Richard's mother that they had not taken time to sign an autograph after a concert. Mrs. Carpenter called her superstar children and demanded they call the fan and apologize. They did.

Friends and classmates can exert a strong influence on a person with an eating disorder. A person who tries and fails to fit into a clique at school or to match the academic or athletic achievements of a popular schoolmate may become depressed and develop an eating disorder. Brothers and sisters can also become part of an eating disorder's creation. When a sibling who excels at sports or in class, or has a specific talent in the arts, is held up as an example to another family member, it doesn't just lower self-esteem. The comparison sets up a rivalry in which the less talented child is doomed to failure. Unrealistic expectations of a child whose talents lie elsewhere is one situation when eating disorders can and do occur.

Another is when the person expects more of himself or herself than the parents do. A student who feels too much pressure to excel may have a false impression of how much is expected. Just talking about those expectations can relieve some of the pressure and start that person on the road to recovery from an eating disorder.

It's not that easy, of course. Eating disorders are complex. Their origins may be deeply buried in the person's subconscious. It takes time, patience, and a lot of questions asked by trained medical professionals to get at the real reasons that anorexia, bulimia, or other eating disorders have developed. The process could take weeks, months, or even more than a year.

Successful recovery also takes the understanding and support of everyone around the affected person. Just as personal relationships can be among the causes of eating disorders, so can they be a vital part of the recovery process and the continued well-being of the person.

9 Caring Intervention and Acceptance

Sometimes it takes a person outside the circle of family and friends to notice when someone has developed an eating disorder and help intervene in its destructive process.

Drew Potthoff is an educator who has had more than one brush with the cruel nature of eating disorders. As principal of the South Beloit Junior High School in South Beloit, Illinois, Potthoff introduced the Student Assistance Program (SAP). He brought the concept from the school district where he worked before moving to South Beloit.

"I was a member of the SAP team and the coordinator for TARGET, an intervention program designed to suppress drug and alcohol use in students, when I met Kelly," Potthoff says. "We'd heard about a party involving drugs and alcohol, and Kelly admitted she'd been at the party."

As Potthoff talked to Kelly, he says he began to realize she had some underlying problems. According to her files, Kelly was a three-sport athlete

85

and cheerleader as well as a good student. But for the six months prior to the party, he explains, it seemed all that was beginning to unravel. Her grades were slipping, and her participation in athletic programs was less than usual.

"Kelly admitted being at the party and drinking a little plus trying some other things," Potthoff says. "She wasn't suspended because she volunteered the information about her involvement. But at the same time, she mentioned struggling with her parents about the pressures and high expectations they were placing on her."

Potthoff says that at the time he couldn't quite put his finger on it, but he believed something more was going on with Kelly. He asked her about using drugs and she said she didn't do drugs. He tried to get her to talk her problems out with the district's guidance counselor, but that failed as well.

It wasn't long before Potthoff learned about another party that involved drugs and alcohol and heard that Kelly had been present at that one, too. This time when he talked to Kelly, she broke down and cried.

"She told me she couldn't go on any more, that the pressure was too much," Potthoff says. "'I'm making myself sick,' she said, and I asked her what she meant. When she admitted eating, then forcing herself to throw up, I knew right away what was going on with Kelly. She was in the early stages of bulimia."

Potthoff says it struck him as very odd that Kelly was behaving much in the same way some groups of women college students had when he was in school. "They would hold what they called 'scarf and barf' parties," Potthoff explains. "It sounds absolutely gross, but the objective was to eat and drink as much as possible, then vomit it up and start all over again. I have to wonder now how many of those students actually had undiagnosed bulimia."

Bulimia is difficult to notice because its symptoms are much more subtle than anorexia, Potthoff says. It was vital to look for the really little things, the subtle changes that signal illness. (You read about those symptoms in chapter three.) "I called Kelly's mother and suggested she take Kelly to a doctor right away," Potthoff says. "The mother said they'd try to handle the problem themselves, but I convinced her they all needed professional help."

Potthoff says his experiences with students' eating disorders indicated that using alcohol and drugs, in combination with anorexia and bulimia, is a way some teens try to deal with stress, pressure, and what they perceive as the requirement by their parents to be perfect.

"It's a vicious cycle, especially when they smoke marijuana," Potthoff says. "Using marijuana makes them hungry, then they eat and drink, then they make themselves sick. If it weren't for my SAP training and being able to gain Kelly's confidence, I don't believe the bulimia would have stopped when it did."

The reason he recognized Kelly's eating disorder so quickly, Potthoff adds, is that he'd already helped another student who was going through similar problems. That time, though, the student was male.

"Johnny was a linebacker on the football team," Potthoff says. "When he was a sophomore, he played varsity. One day, some of his classmates told me he had gotten sick during his physical education class, which was immediately after his lunch break."

When he talked to Johnny, Potthoff says, Johnny admitted he had drunk a little beer at lunch and had eaten too much, so he had thrown up. The possibility that Johnny might have an eating disorder such as anorexia or bulimia didn't occur to him, Potthoff added, because he believed that only young women developed those disorders.

"I really didn't think too much about it until his parents called me during holiday break," Potthoff says. "Johnny had a bedroom in their basement. They had found him in his bathroom, sitting on the floor and crying. He'd lost a lot of weight, and they were shocked to find that he had vomited into a shoebox in an effort to hide what he was doing."

Johnny told Potthoff that he wanted to play a different position from linebacker. Careful questioning in response to this comment revealed that Johnny was comparing himself to his older brother, who was a sports star at school and had a lot of girlfriends.

"Johnny was shy and built heavier than his brother, so that was the real reason he felt less popular. He told me he looked like a fat slob. It just wasn't true," Potthoff explained. "Johnny weighed 170 pounds, down from the 240 pounds he normally weighed. He told me the same thing Kelly said years later, that he just couldn't go on anymore with what was happening to him."

Johnny was anorexic, Potthoff says. When he got too hungry to stand it anymore, he would turn to bulimic behavior, eating a huge amount of food and then vomiting it up. As a result of the unhealthy cycle he was trapped in, Johnny had become severely depressed. He was hospitalized for treatment for three weeks.

"If Johnny hadn't gotten help when he did, I don't know what would have happened to him," Potthoff says.

You need to dig deep to find the real problems underneath the eating disorder, Potthoff says. Students sometimes came to him saying they'd decided to quit school and get a job, or made other choices involving drugs and alcohol. These actions were all efforts to avoid dealing with the real problem: that they felt the need to succeed beyond the level they believed they were capable of reaching. Or they were comparing themselves unfavorably to people they admired and wanted to emulate.

"In many cases, the perception they had of what was expected of them was very different from what their parents really expected," Potthoff notes.

In-school programs such as SAP rely on extensive training of teachers, guidance counselors, and administrative staff. These people, who work closely with students, are trained to be especially observant of minor changes in attitude, emotion, attention span, and physical well-being. When they see something in a student's actions or attitude that concerns them, they fill out a referral form. The form is submitted to a trained team of SAP leaders that includes administrative staff, teachers, and school board members. The school nurse is also a part of the evaluation team. If the situation warrants further attention or some sort of intervention, the student's parents are informed and brought into the process. A decision is then made on how best to help the student.

Many school-based programs like SAP, including peer mentoring and peer mediation, have proven valuable in giving every student the best possible chance of fulfilling his or her potential.

Linda says she wished now that her school friends or a teacher had noticed something was wrong with her and had taken the risk to do something about it.

"There's a pretty good chance that, for most of the time I was bulimic, I wasn't ready to listen," Linda says. "But what if the dentist hadn't insisted that Mom take me to a doctor? Would someone else have had the wisdom and courage to intervene on my behalf? I wonder at times what would have happened to me if . . . well, it really scares me to even think it."

Wendy expressed the same feelings. "My friends must have known something was terribly wrong with me in school," Wendy says. "The teachers must have, too. I wasn't capable of helping myself at the time, so why didn't someone else? Or was I expecting too much of them?"

That's a tough question. Here's another one: What would you do if you had a good friend who began to show symptoms of an eating disorder?

There are a number of possible plans of action. You are the only person who can decide how to handle the knowledge that a friend has an eating disorder. One approach you could try is talking to the person about the changes you've noticed. Express your concern for the person's health and happiness.

If you do learn that the person has some type of eating disorder, never promise to help keep it a secret. Even if your friend begs you not to tell, the best thing you can do is to talk with someone in authority whom you trust about what you've learned. That person may be a medical professional, a minister, a teacher, a guidance counselor, the school nurse, or one of your parents. Whoever you talk to, get help as soon as you can.

Your friend may become extremely angry with you. Don't be surprised if that happens. It's very hard for someone with an eating disorder to face reality and begin to deal with it. The person may not want to change or have others find out about their eating problems. Ultimately, telling someone about your friend's eating disorder may cost you the friendship. But even if that is the case, the alternative is worse, because not trying to get help for your friend may mean that his or her health and even survival are threatened.

10 Making Friends with Food

Eating disorders are psychological, which means they begin in the mind—in the way we perceive our selves, our problems, and others around us. Addictions are also psychological disorders. When a person is treated for an addiction to drugs or alcohol, he is encouraged to avoid the places and people associated with his addiction. For example, if your friends were heavily involved in cocaine use, you would be advised to stop spending time with them and to end the friendships to save yourself.

The same holds true of alcoholism and smoking. Breaking unhealthy habits such as drinking, smoking, or using drugs means breaking away from the people, places, and routines that you associate with those habits. And full recovery from drug addiction or alcoholism means you can't go back to those situations or places without the risk of slipping back into those unhealthy habits.

But there's an obvious difference with eating disorders. You can stop smoking, drinking, and taking drugs, but you can't stop eating. In fact, with anorexia, not eating is the root of the problem. You can avoid places where people are smoking, drinking, or using drugs, but it would be much more difficult to avoid places and situations where people eat. So, how does a person with an eating disorder recover when he or she can never get away from food? Although most people with eating disorders admit that they think about food all the time, read cookbooks, and plan menus for special occasions, they see food as the enemy. Nutritionists describe this as having an obsession with food.

Just as drugs, cigarettes, or alcohol are masks behind which the real enemies—loss of control, striving for perfection, too much pressure, low self-esteem and poor body image—hide, so too is the way in which people with eating disorders see food.

It may sound funny, but you have to make friends with food. "Recovery from an eating disorder is a three-pronged effort," Kim Rewerts, a registered dietitian, says. "There's a psychologist or psychiatrist working on therapy, a physiological doctor evaluating and supporting the patient's health, and a nutritionist. That's where I come into the picture."

Also a registered dietitian, certified diabetic educator, and eating specialist for Rockford Health Systems in Rockford, Illinois, Rewerts says many of her patients come in on their own with self-diagnosed anorexic or bulimic symptoms; others are referred by their doctors or psychiatrists. "Either way, the first thing I do is assess the person's attitude and determine how his or her disorder is structured so I can organize treatment," Rewerts says. When a patient is in a crisis brought on by an eating disorder, she adds, it's often necessary to hospitalize the person and stabilize his or her physical condition before embarking on a dietary program.

"It's hard to process new information when you're basically trying to survive," Rewerts says. "We have to wait until the person is ready to deal with relearning how to eat." Rewerts explains that her program for outpatients runs between eight and twelve weeks, and focuses on how to eat, not what to eat. Patients see her in her clinic office for one hour each week and are asked to check back in on a regular basis to deal with whatever might have emerged from their ongoing psychological or psychiatric treatments.

"People with eating disorders have lost the knowledge of how to eat," Rewerts says. "They're obsessed with food and want to debate what to eat as a diversion, thus preventing or delaying recovery. To be successful, nutritional training must be done in conjunction with good psychological therapy, which deals with the how and why of the disorder, and not the what."

People caught in the throes of an eating disorder need to learn about hunger, appetite, and satisfaction as well as to trust their bodies, Rewerts says. They also need to know how their bodies drive their needs and when enough is enough. "We don't restrict or try to control what they eat," Rewerts says. "Instead, we focus on eating exercises, and we set goals. They learn to manage their bodies and to be present in the moment, to take charge and gain control of their weight."

There are no tricks to this process, Rewerts

says, nor is it an intellectual exercise. "We want to make them be aware, to make conscious choices and have a positive relationship with food," Rewerts says. "We want them to be able to trust their bodies and to separate eating skills from all the other underlying influences that have brought them to this point."

Rewerts says her most powerful tool is to give patients the ability to follow a clear path on how to eat, and not to focus on what they eat. "They just love to take you there, to the what," Rewerts says. "But their survival depends on doing what they have to do until they learn a better way. I give them the techniques and ability to understand how to feed their bodies right."

Among the goals Rewerts teaches her patients is how to eat in a positive and deliberate fashion. What they eat, however, is entirely up to them. Rewerts also works with her patients to separate all the phobias and anxieties they feel from food itself. She says she empowers them to deal with their insecurities and self-doubt, to become more self-confident, and to focus on the other issues troubling them.

"When my doctor ordered me into the hospital for treatment, a team was formed to help me," Wendy says. "I had a medical doctor to monitor my physical condition and to prescribe any medications or treatment I needed, a psychiatrist to conduct the therapy I needed to get my thinking straight, and a nutritionist. Weird as it may sound, we didn't talk about what to eat, but how to eat."

Wendy explains that her nutritionist worked with her several days each week. In those sessions,

Wendy relearned everything she was taught about food's essential values and the food pyramid in school. In addition, the nutritionist and Wendy developed daily menus based on protein, carbohydrate, fat, vitamin, and mineral content.

"At first I couldn't believe it when she told me we weren't going to focus on what to eat," Wendy says. "I expected her to try to stuff every possible morsel down my throat in an effort to make me gain weight. Of course, that wouldn't have worked. I would have fought that any way I could."

Wendy says she was encouraged to think more about trusting her body and appetite. "After listening to her for several sessions, it began to make sense. After not eating for years, and with the physical damage that I did to my heart and other internal organs, the worst thing I could have done was suddenly dump a lot of heavy food on my poor digestive system."

It took a long time, weeks and months of psychiatric therapy, and repeated nutritional messages before Wendy was ready to act upon what she was learning. Wendy says it was extremely difficult to give up her anorexic behaviors. But when she was ready, she eased into more acceptable eating patterns on the strength of what she had learned from her nutritionist.

Unlike Wendy, Linda didn't have years of habit behind her eating disorder, but it still was hard for her to see food in a positive light. "I love food, don't get me wrong," Linda says. "But eating would take away the one thing in life I wanted most at that time: Justin. I thought about food. I even dreamed about food. Hamburgers dripping with melted cheese, pizza loaded with sausage, strawberry shakes, hot fudge sundaes, all the things I love."

But, Linda added, eating what she loved and craved threw her into a panic, and that sent her to the nearest bathroom. Sometimes, she didn't even leave the restaurant before she vomited up what she had consumed.

"I spent a lot of time arguing with my psychologist about what would happen if I started eating normally," Linda says. "It took months before I was convinced I wouldn't break out in fat the moment I let some of that food stay in my stomach. The mind set and habit had become so much a part of me that my bulimic behavior lasted longer than my romance did."

Like Wendy, Linda spent some of her outpatient recovery program with a dietitian, learning how to eat all over again.

"I learned things about food I'd forgotten, and more information on nutrition than I'd ever had before," Linda says. "Now I understand that I can eat a reasonable, well-balanced diet every day and not worry about gaining weight. I can't honestly say I've made peace with food, but we do have a truce."

Bulimic behavior, including bingeing and purging, was only recognized as a disorder less than twenty years ago, but it's hardly new. The Romans ate tremendous feasts, gorging on rich foods in course after course through hours of dining. When they became too full, they had servants tickle their throats with a feather to cause them to vomit up what they had already eaten so they would have room for more.

This, of course, is more like greed and gluttony than an eating disorder. For Randy, the cycle of bingeing, guilt, starving, and bingeing again evolved through his youth into a full-blown eating disorder.

Medical experts believe that as many as 35 percent of clinically obese people are compulsive overeaters. But all that miserable company didn't make Randy feel any better. What did help was finding a friend, an organization and a plan that gave him the strength to break the cycle.

"Joining Overeaters Anonymous was a revelation for me," Randy says. "My bad eating habits didn't stop overnight, of course. But I found sensible guidelines that I now believe saved my sanity, if not my life. I know how to eat, what to eat, and what situations to avoid. I've learned how to break all those habits I had. Best of all, when I feel as if I want to buy out the nearest candy store or start making excuses to stop by my favorite bakery, I have the support I need as close as the telephone."

Wendy, Linda, and Randy have each learned that in the aftermath of an eating disorder, it is vital to have an eating plan. The plan should be designed to provide maximum nutritional benefit without causing further damage to bodies which have endured months or years of food-related abuse.

Another key to recovery is understanding how food is used by the body and the elements that each type of food provides for the best health.

But most of all, making an ally and friend of food instead of something to be avoided, rejected, or devoured without thought is one of the most important aspects of recovery from any eating disorder.

11

Treatment and Recovery

What happens after a person is diagnosed with an eating disorder varies, depending on how severe the disorder is, the person's physical condition, and how cooperative the person is in the recovery process.

To be successful, treatments must address both the physical and psychological aspects of the eating disorder. People with eating disorders frequently fight treatment, especially treatment for the physical condition. To treat the entire person, medical professionals must convince that person that he or she needs the treatment and then gain willing participation. While the person is receiving psychological therapy, the eating disorder continues and the person's health is in constant jeopardy. The degree to which the person's health and well-being are affected by the eating disorder determines to a large extent how that treatment will be conducted.

But the first and most important concern in treating anorexia and bulimia is the restoration of the person's nutritional and physical health. That's because dehydration (lack of sufficient liquid in the body), starvation (lack of sufficient nutrients in the body), and electrolyte imbalances (too much or not enough of certain chemicals in the brain) can cause serious physical problems or even death.

TREATING ANOREXIA

Eating disorder specialists use a combination of hospitalization, psychotherapy, and pharmacotherapy (prescribing medications that can help in recovery, such as antidepressants) to treat both anorexia and bulimia.

A person whose anorexia nervosa is moderate can be treated on an outpatient basis from a clinic, a hospital, or even a private office. Treatment can take anywhere from weeks to months but seldom lasts as long as a year except for regular follow-up checks, monitoring when necessary, and relapses. But in cases of severe or prolonged anorexia, hospitalization may be the person's best chance at recovery. Anorexia patients are hospitalized when their conditions meet some or all of the following criteria:

1. When a person loses 30 percent of body weight or more over a period of three months, hospitalization to intervene in the destructive process may be necessary. A type of psychiatric treatment known as cognitive behavior therapy often works, though it takes time. In extreme cases, taking care of the patient's physical condition takes precedence over long-term

psychological treatments until the person is stabilized.

2. Hospitalization is recommended if extreme metabolic disturbance has taken place. This means that the person's digestive process and the way the body accepts and uses nutrients have been critically upset. Lack of essential nutrients such as potassium, calcium, iron, and others can cause permanent physical damage in a surprisingly short time.

3. Anytime the anorexic patient is diagnosed with severe depression or is considered a suicide risk in addition to having an eating disorder, hospitalization is the surest way to protect that person's life until other methods of intervention can turn the disorder around.

4. If the patient engages in bulimic behavior and the binge-and-purge cycle becomes severe enough to warrant immediate intervention, hospitalization and twenty-four-hour monitoring may be vital. Some binge-and-purge patterns remain fairly consistent over time, but additional pressures, problems, or severe depression can cause that pattern to short-circuit. Common sense tells us that the more a person binges and purges, the more serious the damage and prognosis become.

5. Some anorexic patients promise to keep their weights at an acceptable point and sign a weight "contract"; when they fall five pounds below that target point, they have broken the contract. Depending on other physical and psychological factors, hospitalization may be warranted to prevent the person from relapsing.

6. When anorexia is only one of the person's physical problems, hospitalization may be necessary. Long-term starvation as the result of anorexia can damage the heart, liver, and kidneys, as well as cause other serious medical conditions. For example, a severe lack of potassium over a long period of time can cause permanent heart damage. Being deprived of iron in the diet can lead to anemia. Every nutrient lost as the result of an eating disorder has an adverse effect on the body.

7. When there is serious concern about the person's mental stability, hospitalization may be required for the person's protection. Doctors may decide that the patient has moved far enough away from reality to require hospitalization. This doesn't mean the patient is insane; rather, the person's perception of the world around him or her has become distorted by the disorder to the point where he or she is safer within a hospital than outside.

8. A crisis due to a family member's illness, divorce, injury, or death may make it necessary to hospitalize an anorexic patient. This is done to insulate him or her from strong emotional reactions that can set back recovery. In these cases, the hospital environment becomes a safety cushion by distancing the patient from the crisis.

9. Repeated confrontation between the person and family members, continued denial of the seriousness of the disorder, or to facilitate the process of family therapy—these are all valid reasons for hospitalization. It's difficult enough to overcome a deep-seated eating disorder without aggravating negative influences. And the patient may not want to accept how serious his or her condition really is. With round-the-clock monitoring and the protective intervention of the medical team treating the patient, the conditions that will best help the person recover can be maintained.

Hospitalization for anorexia involves a wide range of programs applied all at once. Behavioral therapy, family education, group therapy, and even psychotropic (mood-altering) medications are part of the arsenal used to battle anorexia.

Many anorexia patients actively resist admission to a hospital. They continue to deny they have an eating disorder. For the first several weeks of inpatient treatment, they may even make frantic pleas to family and friends to get them released from the hospital. Some even try to escape once they are hospitalized. Wendy was one of those. She admits that even though she realized how much she needed help with her anorexia, she attempted to sign herself out of the hospital.

"I hated being in the hospital. I tried to escape once, by putting a coat on over my hospital gown and sneaking down the back stairwell to the underground garage," Wendy says. "Because I had been anorexic for a long time, I wound up as an inpatient for more than a year. I know now that's unusual. But what isn't unusual is that I still have constant contact with my doctor, several times weekly, after more than five years."

Wendy's not alone, and that's good. The majority of persons treated for anorexia need long-term support after they are discharged from the hospital.

Along with learning how to eat, hospitalized patients are involved in psychotherapy on a daily basis. There are dozens of theories on how to treat anorexia and other eating disorders, but most medical professionals use cognitive behavioral therapy to monitor weight gain, sustain health maintenance, and confront unacceptable eating behaviors. At the same time, therapists study other issues that may be involved in each patient's eating disorder, such as depression or bipolar disorder. Family therapy, which takes a close look at the interpersonal relationships among family members, is also used in the treatment of eating disorders. Understanding those relationships is important to the recovery process, because unresolved issues can complicate recovery in unexpected ways.

Pharmacotherapy, the use of medications to supplement and support psychotherapy, is often a successful part of eating disorder treatment. No magic pill or potion exists that will relieve eating disorder symptoms or get rid of the disorder altogether, but there are a few that can be helpful.

The destructive force of any eating disorder can become so powerful as to sometimes require very aggressive treatment to save the patient's life. One such treatment is electroconvulsive therapy. For a few cases involving anorexia nervosa, especially if it is complicated by the presence of a major depressive disorder, electric shock treatments have proven effective.

TREATING BULIMIA

Treatments for persons recovering from bulimia nervosa are a little different from those for anorexics. Overall, bulimia patients aren't as secretive about their eating disorders as those with anorexia. And because of this, they tend to be more receptive to treatment. Most can be successfully treated on an outpatient basis.

But when eating binges are severe, or if the person has other physical or psychiatric symptoms, such as suicidal tendencies or problems with substance abuse, hospitalization may become vital. Another reason for hospitalization may be extreme purging over a period of time, causing electrolyte imbalances or metabolic disturbances. The bulimic patient's primary doctor must be trusted to use good judgment in whether hospitalization is necessary.

For bulimia patients, it is important to regulate both eating habits and weight. Once the person is more stable physically, control is gradually returned. Behavior modification based on the person's weight and eating patterns is carefully structured. All of this is backed by long-term therapy and medical follow-up programs.

"One of the goals my doctor set was the development of self-control and judgment," Linda says. "Of course, I thought I already was in control, but I learned that wasn't true."

Linda adds that group therapy really helps a person with bulimia understand how the disorder affects the way he or she thinks. "When you sit there and hear someone else use all your excuses, it's a real eye-opener," Linda says. "Group therapy is great support. We've all been there, done that. You find you can't kid fellow bulimics. They know all about it, and because they've learned to care a lot about what happens to themselves and fellow sufferers, they don't let anyone else get away with the same baloney they pulled."

Antidepressants can be used to help bulimia patients recover, especially if they don't respond well to psychotherapy alone. Fluoxetine, better known as Prozac, is one of the antidepressants often prescribed for treatment. There are also a few others used on a limited basis.

Self-management is one of the key elements in recovery. Again, although it takes medical professionals, family, and friends to help a person with an eating disorder get better, only the patient can decide to start the recovery process and continue it.

With that in mind, here are the elements that are

necessary for a person with bulimia or anorexia to truly recover:

- ⊙ The patient has to take part fully in the treatment plan and complete any nutritional, medical, and therapeutic programs assigned to him or her.

- ⊙ The person must be able to function independently in day-to-day living and must show that he or she can cope with any problems or emotional stress that life brings.

- ⊙ The patient must keep all appointments on a timely basis with the medical team monitoring his or her maintenance program; the patient must never lie or hold back information when reporting.

- ⊙ The person has to keep his or her weight within five pounds of the assigned target weight; if the weight level begins to drop for any reason, the person must immediately report the loss and ask for help.

TREATING COMPULSIVE OVEREATING

Treatment for compulsive overeating is, naturally, different from treatment for anorexia and bulimia. Still, group therapy is a viable method of supporting compulsive overeaters through the tough job of permanently changing how they perceive food and the world around them.

Groups such as Weight Watchers and Take Off Pounds Sensibly (TOPS) help those who have recognized their need to reduce their weight and keep it off. Overeaters Anonymous and programs like it go one step further. In OA, group therapy based on the twelve steps developed by the founder of Alcoholics Anonymous helps individuals learn to control their eating habits, binges, and even depression. Programs such as Overcoming Overeating help compulsive eaters focus on the underlying causes of their behavior and learn to listen to their body's needs and signals instead of trying to stuff them back inside with food.

Even compulsive overeaters may require an initial period of hospitalization to intervene in their disorder and to treat the strong guilt feelings or deep depression that often accompany this eating disorder. "I don't know for certain, but I feel I was very close to the point where I would have had to be hospitalized for compulsive overeating," Randy says. "I'm only in my late twenties, but with the weight I carried, and the types of foods I ate, sooner or later, I would have had a heart attack, a stroke, or have fallen and broken something."

Randy admits he never would have gone to a doctor or clinic to help him deal with his compulsive overeating disorder. "My attitude toward my weight created a wicked combination," Randy says when asked why. "First of all, I was ashamed of my weight, but I felt that seeking professional help was an admission that I wasn't in control. I wasn't, of course, but I didn't want to see that, or hear it, either. After Mary talked to me about Overeaters Anonymous, I thought about it seriously and decided if I was going to confront my eating disorder, I was going to do it on my terms."

Any professional medical treatment for compulsive overeating disorder must be conducted on two levels to be successful. Clinical depression and compulsive overeating must be addressed at the same time to break the interdependent pattern the patient has developed, in which depressive behavior fuels bouts of compulsive eating and vice versa. This usually involves working simultaneously on diet, behavior modification, nutritional education, exercise, antidepressants when necessary, and a long-range maintenance plan.

Weight control techniques that doctors and nutritionists typically work on with compulsive overeaters are as follows:

- ⊙ Patients keep a food diary to keep them actively aware of how, when, where, what, and sometimes why they eat as they do.

- ⊙ Healthier eating habits are established. For example, all food is eaten in the same place, with the patient sitting down comfortably. Reading, watching television, and other distracting activities are discouraged during the time the person is eating.

- ⊙ Common-sense rules such as portion control, keeping food stored out of sight, and not going to the grocery store when the patient is hungry are stressed to help the recovering compulsive eater control his or her urges.

⊙ Positive ways to deal with loneliness, anxiety, boredom, anger, frustration, and other emotions that don't involve eating are developed. Rewards other than food treats for successes are also discussed.

⊙ Incremental goals that slowly change eating habits for the better are initiated, with the understanding they will take time and a lot of hard work.

THE RISK OF RELAPSE

Relapse is always a danger with eating disorders. Anytime there is the slightest hint that a person is returning to destructive eating habits, it is vital to contact the medical team that has helped the person in the recovery process immediately.

For persons who have been successfully recovering from eating disorders, the symptoms of relapse are very similar. A person who gains or loses five pounds or more from the maintenance weight range that has been determined for him or her is in danger of relapse. Increases in addictive behavior, regardless of whether that involves food, exercise, drugs, or alcohol, are also clear signs of trouble. A sudden or sharp decrease in appetite or ability to eat is another symptom that a recovering person may relapse. So is an episode of purging, along with renewed use of laxatives, diuretics, diet pills and enemas. Another less obvious sign is a marked change in the person's sleeping patterns; the person either sleeps more than usual or suddenly is unable to sleep.

Whether the recovery process is conducted through hospitalization, under an outpatient treatment program or, more rarely, on one's own, it's never easy. Recovery is not like recovering from a physical illness, with a prescribed method of treatment that results in a permanent cure.

Support by medical professionals, family, friends and coworkers is essential to help a person not only recover from an eating disorder, but to maintain that recovery level for a lifetime.

The Many Faces of Eating Disorder Treatment

In the early 1980s, when many medical professionals first began to pay attention to anorexia and bulimia, they tried to find a single, fundamental cause on which to base treatment.

As they learned more about anorexia and bulimia, as well as binge-purge syndrome, compulsive exercising, compulsive overeating, and muscle dysmorphia, they began to realize that there was no one simple answer to solving the riddles that eating disorders presented.

Anorexics believe they are in complete control, and bulimics believe they are completely out of control. Control is always an issue, whether or not the person with the disorder believes this. Repressed anger and other difficult emotions play their part. So does denial.

In the past two decades, dozens of different methods of treating eating disorders have evolved. All of them are more or less effective and are primarily founded on therapists' experience, education, and convictions.

As noted earlier, many treatment programs are based on cognitive behavior therapy. The dictionary defines cognition as the process of knowing in the broadest sense, including perception, memory, and judgment, as well as the results of such a process. In the case of eating disorders, then, cognitive behavior therapy is aimed at making patients aware not only of the reality of their conditions, but also the process by which they developed their eating disorders, the reasons they developed them, and how to assess their current physical and psychological state honestly.

Interpersonal therapy, group psychotherapy and psycho-education are additional tools therapists use to dislodge eating disorder behavior and replace it with healthy concepts. But although all of the different treatment methods work, no single method works in all cases.

An eating disorder can be looked at as if it were an apple. Imagine that you are a therapist. In your hand is this bright, beautiful red apple. Cognitive behavior therapy, group therapy, education, and reason are what you, as a therapist, are going to use to get at the core of this apple.

You can't see inside the apple—your patient—yet. You don't know what lies beneath the skin, how sweet and juicy that apple is, or whether there are bad spots or even a worm. And you don't know what hides at its core, either—how many dark seeds exist that hold the origins of the eating disorder. As an eating disorder treatment specialist, you must first break through the hard outer peel—the emotions, anxiety, fear, and false perceptions that keep you from penetrating into the first layers.

To pare away this level, you may use antidepressants and tranquilizers to calm the patient, to ease the process of psychological treatment, and help the patient feel better about himself or herself during the process. You do this realizing that you have only scratched the surface, and that medications will only make the process of treating an eating disorder less painful and more productive.

Now you delicately begin to scrape away the layers of low self-esteem, poor body image, fear of losing control—all the thick pulp that hides the kernels of agony that are causing the eating disorder. It takes time and patience; sometimes it feels as if you have made no progress at all. Other times, it seems as if the patient, like some strange variety of apple, has regrown some of those deceptively soft layers overnight.

The apple resists this entire process. Although on some level it knows how necessary the process is, the patient doesn't want its core exposed with all the pain and uncertainty it has kept buried beneath that thick, sweet pulp for so long. But slowly you approach the truth beneath all the misconceptions. You begin to uncover, one by one, the small, hard seeds at the core of the disorder. Some of these can be labeled easily: sexual or physical abuse; fear of failure and of not living up to the expectations of others; fear of not feeling in control of at least one aspect of life; anxieties about being fat; fears of failing to live up to role models; guilt; and depression. Others might surprise you. There are almost as many reasons, and combinations of reasons, for developing an eating disorder as there are people suffering from them. So it makes sense that there are many different approaches to treating eating disorders, depending on how and why the therapist has developed his or her unique therapies.

One such therapist is Peggy Claude-Pierre, who founded and directs the Montreaux Clinic in Canada. Author of *The Secret Language of Eating Disorders,* Claude-Pierre developed her program after first one teenage daughter, then a second one became anorexic. Helping her daughters recover from anorexia nervosa convinced Claude-Pierre that successful therapy must go beyond simple behavior modification to uncover the underlying causes. And she began to believe that people could be genetically prone to developing eating disorders as well. Claude-Pierre now provides procedures based on her theories to counselors and the caregivers who are helping family members overcome eating disorders.

Rebecca Manley founded the Massachusetts Eating Disorders Association based on even more personal experiences. By age eight, Manley was already on the road to years of dealing with anorexia. Feeling that she was fatter than her classmates, she became a compulsive exerciser and admitted to stealing money to buy laxatives and water pills to keep her weight down. When Manley finally checked into an eating disorder clinic, she learned her problem wasn't food, but feelings.

Determined that others shouldn't go through what she did, Manley earned a master's degree in family studies and counseling. In 1994, she started the Massachusetts Eating Disorders Association and began helping others. "I didn't have anorexia because I wanted to look like Barbie," Manley says. "It was how I expressed my pain. I try to teach kids that it's okay to talk about their feelings. If someone had taught me how, I might never have had anorexia. I want kids to know that."

Some therapies involve getting in touch with feelings and digging into the underlying causes of eating disorders. Others assist recovery in a "stepped" program similar to the one used by Alcoholics Anonymous and Overeaters Anonymous. Treatment of eating disorders through theories developed at Rogers Memorial Hospital in Oconomowoc, Wisconsin, involves careful listening, respect, and seeing what Dr. Thomas J. Shiltz calls the "positive intent" of the eating disorder. Shiltz believes recovery is more about redirecting energy and redefining purpose, instead of eliminating eating disorder symptoms.

"I know when I was hospitalized that the other patients had doctors with conflicting theories of how to treat eating disorders," Wendy says. "We talked about the differences occasionally. I often wonder now how some of them would have worked for me. But what I really wish is that the newer programs were available when I was diagnosed and treated. What I went through, and my doctor with me, was very hard. I'll always wonder if a different approach would have been better, or would have worked more quickly."

RETURNING TO HEALTH

When anorexics start eating again, the changes are dramatic. All of their basic bodily functions including sleep patterns, heart rates, body temperature and energy improve incrementally in pace with their food intake.

Sometimes all it takes to turn a person with an eating disorder around is the realization of what may be lost if the condition continues.

"I was talking to an anorexic patient in group therapy one day," Linda says. "She says she began recovering the moment her therapist told her she might never have children if she continued starving herself. Eventually starting a family became extremely important to her, more important than holding on to her anorexia."

Finding the key to what will help a person with an eating disorder let go of that behavior in favor of something more important is another method of treatment that works on some patients.

Linda notes that the one thing that helped her more than anything else was finally understanding that being thin wouldn't automatically make life better or bring the things she most wanted.

"We talked. Boy, did we talk," Linda says of her therapy sessions. "I talked around and around the real issue, that being skinny wouldn't guarantee my boyfriend's affections or anything else, for that matter."

Linda says her recovery process for bulimia nervosa reminded her of a still, deep lake. "I kept testing the waters with a toe, then backing away," Linda adds. "It took time and a lot of convincing before I was willing to wade into the water, and even longer to rediscover I knew how to swim."

Randy found what he needed most in the company of people who were recovering from compulsive overeating: understanding, compassion, insight, and support.

"I know there are radical physical treatments for

people who weighed as much as I did and more," Randy says. "Having my stomach stapled or partially removed wasn't an option for me. When I finally decided I needed to deal with my overeating problem, I wanted to do it on my own terms and without artificial means."

That meant no surgery, pills, liquid diets, or fasts for Randy. He says he had several reasons for his decision, including the lack of sufficient insurance coverage for that type of treatment through his employment. Eating disorder treatment can be very expensive, and not all aspects of it are covered by standard insurance policies, including what may be determined as elective surgery.

Instead, Randy decided to count on members of Overeaters Anonymous, who were in the process of recovering from compulsive overeating, to help him through the difficult process.

"It's taken years to bring my weight down and change the way I look at both food and life," Randy says. "I still have bad days. But now I have the support of a group of people who know firsthand what's involved in recovering from compulsive overeating. That's made a tremendous difference in my outlook, as well as my future."

AN IMPROVING PICTURE

Each person facing an eating disorder has more treatment options now than ever before. The process of recognizing that an eating disorder exists, then finding the right therapeutic approach and philosophy to start the patient on the road to recovery, has evolved remarkably since the early 1980s.

Medical professionals who regularly work with eating disorder patients stress that it is important for the patient not to avoid healthcare specialists. Finding a psychiatrist or therapist who can approach treatment in a respectful yet realistic manner can make all the difference. For those who are not ready for treatment, a health-care professional can at least help to keep them alive and supported until they are ready for therapy.

Regardless of which theory and methodology a patient chooses to help overcome an eating disorder, the odds of a lasting recovery are better than ever before.

13 Getting Help

"**I** think I'm fat."

"I'm a horrible person. I must deserve this."

"It's my own fault."

"My problems don't matter."

These are just some of the things people who have developed eating disorders say about themselves and their personal worth. If you are a person with healthy self-esteem and a positive self-image, you might find it hard to take comments such as these seriously. But when the person who continues to put him- or herself down like this also displays many of the symptoms that signal an eating disorder, which you've read about in past chapters, you may have to make a decision about what to do to help.

You have learned in this book that overcoming low self-esteem and unrealistic body images associated with eating disorders isn't simple. Unlike physical illnesses, eating disorders are complex psychological disorders that require intensive, individualized treatment. So how do you, as a caring person, help someone you feel has developed an eating disorder?

First, the more you know, the better equipped you will be to help if and when you come in contact with a friend, family member, coworker, or acquaintance who is struggling with an eating disorder. Very few people have successfully recovered from an eating disorder on their own. It takes the support and understanding of family, friends, coworkers, teachers, coaches, or other concerned people to reinforce the clinically-based recovery program. And eating disorder sufferers need the combined professional help of a team of doctors, dietitians, and psychiatrists or psychologists to work through the layers of denial and low self-esteem to find what may have caused the eating disorder.

"I wish the people closest to me had known about anorexia when I was in the early stages," Wendy says. "It would have saved years of pain and grief, not only for me but for my family as well. My advice is, if you even suspect someone you care about has an eating disorder, don't wait. Get help for them right away, even if it makes them angry."

Wendy stresses that people trying to help someone with an eating disorder should not be surprised or frightened away from helping if the person reacts angrily. Especially in cases of anorexia, the patient may strongly deny that he or she has an eating disorder. And that person may not want help—even though you can see that he or she desperately needs it right away.

If you are unable to make the person listen to reason and seek help, the next-best step is to find a responsible adult or person with more influence and talk to that person about how to find help.

And if you're hesitant to intervene because you're unsure the person has an eating disorder, you'll find a wealth of information from a variety of resources. Read up, check up, follow up. That way, if nothing else, you may be able to set your mind at ease about the person's condition. Fortunately, there are many definitive books and magazine articles, as well as non-profit organizations, dedicated to providing the latest information on eating disorders. New resources for information and counseling are instantly accessible on the Internet as well. Your community, school district, or college library should have a wide variety of books and magazine articles available on the many aspects of eating disorders. If you need help, you can ask the library's research and customer service departments. These same people will be able to access articles and Web sites online for you or help you use library Internet services to research eating disorders.

"I know my friends in school must have suspected something was wrong with me," Linda says. "I believe they were afraid to interfere with my romance. And my boyfriend must have known. So much for what I believed were caring relationships. I still wonder how long I would have suffered if my dentist hadn't said something to Mom."

Linda says that even though she knows now that bulimia patients are more receptive to treatment than people with anorexia, she would have resisted help at the time. But, she adds, it wouldn't have been much longer before her health deteriorated to the point where even she would have recognized her need for intervention.

"Take the chance, that's what I'd advise," Linda

says. "Your friend or relative might get angry, but in time he or she will accept the fact that you cared enough to brave that anger. Even if he or she never accepts it, you'll still feel better about yourself than if you let someone you cared about continue to hurt himself or herself, or even die."

Randy points out that it took a lot of guts for his friend Mary to confront him about his weight problem and the possible solution. "I wasn't angry as much as I was hurt," Randy says. "And that seems so silly and superficial now, because deep down, I knew I had an eating disorder. I knew that if I didn't deal with my compulsive overeating soon, the day would come when all that fat, cholesterol, and strain on my internal organs would overcome my basic good health."

It took the thoughtful, caring intervention of someone Randy trusted to turn his eating disorder around. Now that he's recovering, Mary's friendship has been supplemented by that of others Randy has met at Overeaters Anonymous, providing an ongoing network of support similar to the monitoring and consistent contact Wendy and Linda have with their therapists.

After you've researched eating disorders by reading this book and by finding additional information in local libraries, support organizations, and on the Internet, take your concerns to the person you feel has an eating disorder in a calm, caring manner.

If that doesn't help, or if you are unable to break through to the person one-on-one, find help through a family member, minister, school administrator, teacher, school nurse, or some other person in authority who has the influence to break the cycle of eating disorder behaviorism and start the person on the way to recovery.

You can also contact any of the organizations listed in Where to Go for Help at the end of this book for more information. Remember, help is out there.

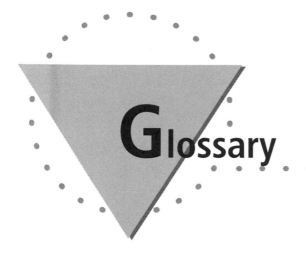

Glossary

anorexia nervosa An eating disorder in which one intentionally starves oneself.

binge To consume large amounts of food, often in secret and usually without control.

binge-eating disorder An eating disorder, similar to compulsive eating, in which a person eats large quantities of food all at once on a regular (but not daily) basis.

binge-purge syndrome A syndrome that is similar to bulimia in which a person frequently eats extremely large quantities of food and then purges them. People with binge-purge syndrome tend to be slightly overweight.

body dysmorphic disorder (BDD) A disorder in which people focus on a real or imagined physical flaw so much that it affects their behavior. People with BDD are unable to perceive their appearance correctly.

body image The way in which people see their bodies, their physical selves.

bulimia nervosa An eating disorder in which one eats normal or large amounts of food and then rids the body of the food by either forcing oneself to vomit, abusing laxatives or diuretics, taking enemas, or exercising obsessively.

calorie A unit to measure the energy-producing value of food.

compulsive eating An eating disorder marked by uncontrollable eating of large amounts of food.

compulsive exercise syndrome An eating disorder in which a person exercises excessively, often for several hours a day, in order to use any calories he or she has taken in. Also called exercise addiction.

denial Refusing to admit or face the truth or reality of a situation.

depression A disorder of mood in which a person has unusually sad feelings persisting over a long period of time.

deprive To withhold something from or take something away.

disordered eating Attitudes and behaviors toward food and eating that do not meet the definition of a recognized eating disorder but still affect a person's overall mental or physical health.

diuretics Medications that increase the frequency and amount of urination. People with certain types of eating disorders may take excessively large quantities of diuretics as a way of purging calories from their bodies.

eating disorder Any problem with food that severely disrupts a person's life.

inpatient A patient who is treated and remains in a hospital or a clinic for treatment.

internalize To bottle up problems or emotions.

laxatives Medications that are normally used to treat constipation but that bulimics and other eating disorder sufferers take in excessively large quantities in order to purge food from their bodies.

muscle dysmorphia An unhealthy preoccupation with building muscles. People with muscle dysmorphia may be very muscular but perceive themselves as physically weak.

obsessive Excessive to the point of being unreasonable.

outpatient A patient in a clinic or hospital who does not live in the hospital but visits on a regular basis for treatment.

overachiever A person who strives for success beyond what is expected.

psychiatrist A doctor who is trained to treat and counsel people with mental, emotional, or behavioral disorders.

purge To rid the body of food in an unnatural way, usually by vomiting or overusing laxatives.

self-esteem Confidence in or satisfaction with oneself; self-respect.

self-image A person's sense of himself or herself including both physical and personality characteristics.

therapy Various types of treatment of emotional and psychological problems.

Where to Go for Help

American Anorexia/Bulimia Association, Inc.
(AABA)
165 West 46th Street, Suite 1108
New York, NY 10036
(212) 575-6200
Web site: http://members.aol.com/amanbu

American College of Sports Medicine
c/o Public Information Office
P.O. Box 1440
Indianapolis, IN 46206-1440
(317) 637-9200
Web site: http://www.a1.com/sportsmed

Anorexia Nervosa and Related Eating Disorders
(ANRED)
P.O. Box 5102
Eugene, OR 97405
(541) 344-1144
Web site: http://www.anred.com

Center for the Study of Anorexia and Bulimia
c/o The Institute for Contemporary Psychotherapy
1841 Broadway, 4th Floor
New York, NY 10023
(212) 333-3444
Web site: http://www.icpnyc.org/treatment/csab.html

Council on Size and Weight Discrimination
P.O. Box 305
Mount Marion, NY 12456
(914) 679-1209
Fax: (914) 679-1206

Eating Disorders Awareness and Prevention (EDAP)
603 Stewart Street, Suite 603
Seattle, WA 98101
(206) 382-3587
Web site: http://members.aol.com/edapinc

The Eating Disorder Connection
(900) 737-4044
($.99 per minute)

Gurze Books
P.O. Box 2238
Carlsbad, CA 92018-9883
(800) 756-7533
Web site: http://www.gurze.com

Helping to End Eating Disorders
9620 Church Avenue
Brooklyn, NY 11212
(718) 240-6451
(718) 934-3853
Web site: http://www.eatingdis.com

National Association of Anorexia Nervosa and Associated Disorders (ANAD)
P.O. Box 7
Highland Park, IL 60035
Hotline: (847) 831-3438
Web site: http://members.aol.com/anad20/index.html

National Eating Disorders Organization (NEDO)
6655 South Yale Avenue
Tulsa, OK 74136
(918) 481-4044
Web site: http://www.laureate.com

Overeaters Anonymous (OA)
P.O. Box 44020
Rio Rancho, NM 87174
(505) 891-2664
Web site: http://www.overeatersanonymous.org

WEB SITES

APA Online
http://www.psych.org
Comprehensive basic information on eating disorders, treatments, medications, and additional resources.

Arlington Town Online
http://www.townonline.com

Ask the Dietitian
http://www.dietitian.com/bulimia.html

Concerned Counseling
http://www.concernedcounseling.com

In addition to providing up-to-date basic information on eating disorders, Concerned Counseling has chat rooms and bulletin boards, first-hand stories of people who have faced eating disorders and recovered, and more.

Eating Disorders Checklist
http://www.umn.edu/hlthserv/counseling/
        eating_disorder.html

Eating Disorders in Males
http://www.mhsource.com/edu/psytimes/p950942.html

Healing Hearts Consulting and Counseling
http://www.worldramp.net
Information and a schedule of workshops on eating disorders and related topics.

National Institute of Mental Health—Eating Disorders.
http://www.nimh.nih.gov/publicat/eatdis.htm

Something Fishy
http://www.something-fishy.org
Something Fishy has extensive information, including case histories, on-line support, editorials, volunteer support systems, and more.

University of Florida Counseling Center
Body Acceptance and Eating Disorders
http://www.ufsa.ufl.edu/Counsel/text.html

For Further Reading

Bode, Janet. *Food Fight: A Guide to Eating Disorders for Pre-Teens and Their Parents.* New York: Simon & Schuster, 1997.

Boskind-White, Marlen, et al. *Bulimarexia: The Binge/Purge Cycle.* New York: W.W. Norton & Co., 1991.

Bruch, Hilde. *Eating Disorders: Obesity, Anorexia Nervosa, and the Person Within.* New York: Basic Books, 1985.

Burby, Liz. *Bulimia Nervosa: The Secret Cycle of Bingeing and Purging.* New York: Rosen Publishing Group, 1998.

Chernin, Kim. *The Hungry Self: Women, Eating and Identity.* New York: HarperCollins, 1994.

Chiu, Christina. *Eating Disorder Survivors Tell Their Stories.* New York: Rosen Publishing Group, 1998.

Claude-Pierre, Peggy. *The Secret Language of Eating Disorders.* New York: Times Books, 1997.

Cooper, Peter J. *Bulimia Nervosa and Binge Eating: A Guide to Recovery.* New York: New York University Press, 1995.

Fairburn, Christopher G. and G. Terence Wilson, eds. *Binge Eating: Nature, Assessment, and Treatment.* New York: Guilford Press, 1993.

Fodor, Viola. *Desperately Seeking Self: An Inner Guidebook for People with Eating Problems.* Carlsbad, CA: Gurze Books, 1997.

Griffiths, Sian, and Jennifer Wallace, eds. *Consuming Passions: Food in the Age of Anxiety.* New York: St. Martin's Press, Inc., 1998.

Hall, Lindsey. *Bulimia: A Guide for Family and Friends.* San Francisco: Jossey-Bass, Inc. Publishers, 1992.

———, et al. *Bulimia: A Guide to Recovery: Understanding & Overcoming the Binge-Purge Syndrome.* Carlsbad, CA: Gurze Books, 1992.

———, and Monika Ostroff. *Anorexia Nervosa: A Guide to Recovery.* Carlsbad, CA: Gurze Books, 1998.

Hornbacher, Marya. *Wasted: A Memoir of Anorexia and Bulimia.* New York: HarperCollins, 1998.

Hutchinson, Marcia Germaine. *Transforming Body Image.* Freedom, CA: The Crossing Press, 1988.

Levenkron, Steven. *The Best Little Girl in the World.* New York: Warner Books, 1981.

Robbins, Paul R. *Anorexia and Bulimia.* Springfield, NJ: Enslow Publishers, 1998.

Roth, Geneen. *Breaking Free from Compulsive Eating.* New York: Plume Co., 1993.

Smith, Erica. *Anorexia Nervosa: When Food Is the Enemy.* New York: Rosen Publishing Group, 1998.

Treasure, Janet. *Anorexia Nervosa: A Survival Guide for Family, Friends, and Sufferers.* Mahwah, NJ: Lawrence Earlbaum Associates, Inc., 1997.

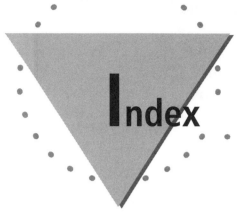

Index